Battleground
THE CHANNEL PORTS

BOULOGNE

20 GUARDS BRIGADE'S
FIGHTING DEFENCE - MAY 1940

Photograph previous page: An abandoned Allied anti-aircraft gun on the harbour front. Bundesarchiv, Koblenz

Battleground Europe
THE CHANNEL PORTS

BOULOGNE

20 GUARDS BRIGADE'S
FIGHTING DEFENCE - MAY 1940

Jon Cooksey

Foreword by Sir Beville Stanier Bt

LEO COOPER

For Heather and Georgia

Other books by Jon Cooksey:

Calais –A Fight to the Finish
(2000 Battleground series)
and
Barnsley Pals
History of the 13th and 14th Battalions,
York and Lancaster Regiment, 1914-1918
(1986)

Published by
LEO COOPER
an imprint of
Pen & Sword Books Limited
47 Church Street, Barnsley, South Yorkshire S70 2AS
Copyright © Jon Cooksey, 2002

ISBN 0 85052 814 3

A CIP catalogue of this book is available
from the British Library

Printed by CPI UK

*For up-to-date information on other titles produced under the Leo Cooper
imprint, please telephone or write to:*
Pen & Sword Books Ltd, FREEPOST SF5, 47 Church Street
Barnsley, South Yorkshire S70 2AS
Telephone 01226 734555

CONTENTS

FOREWORD
by
Sir Beville Stanier Bt

I can remember, very clearly, at the age of six, the moment when my mother said to me, 'Your father's safe and he's back from Boulogne.' Of course at such a young age, I had no real idea of what he and the men of 2nd Battalion, Welsh Guards, of whom he was in command, had been through in those latter days of May 1940. The battles that took place then, around both Boulogne and Calais, have been a somewhat forgotten episode for the greater British public by comparison with Dunkirk and indeed in subsequent years have tended to recede still further from our collective memory.

My father held the dual distinction of being one of the last British commanding officers to leave continental Europe in 1940 before the Fall of France and one of the first to return four years later on D-Day as a Brigade Commander. He landed on Gold Beach on 6 June 1944, near Arromanches, where his personal memorial lies next to the sea wall in the town square. His 231 Infantry Brigade fought right through France and, ironically, back up to the northern channel ports from where he had been so unceremoniously ejected over four years earlier.

He did not talk much about the war afterwards, although he wrote occasional articles for the regimental magazine. It was only at a late stage in his ninety-six year life that he was eventually interviewed and a tape was recorded in which he gave an account of his personal experiences in Boulogne and his recollections of those frantic hours. It was only then that I began to understand the tension and the drama of the withdrawal and subsequent evacuation, under fire, from Boulogne harbour.

Now, with this book, Jon Cooksey has illuminated the whole episode for his readers. He shows how this battle was fought with much discipline in the face of overwhelming odds and without adequate support and resources. He writes from both Allied and German perspectives, bringing the action to life in a fast moving and dramatic style. It is much enhanced by the first-hand memories of both British and German veterans.

The audacious advance of General Guderian's XIX *Panzerkorps* is described in a thrilling way, reminiscent of Rommel's feats in North Africa. Equally exciting are the experiences of the men of 20 Guards Brigade as they are forced back into the town of Boulogne from which most, but not all, escaped back to England. This book adds a new dimension to those uncertain days and complements his account of the 1940 battle for Calais previously chronicled.

INTRODUCTION

It is almost two years since the publication of *Calais – A Fight to the Finish – May 1940* and in many ways this book could be seen as its companion volume. Some of the events which unfold on these pages were taking place at the same time as the bitter fighting for Calais, then not much more than a forty minute truck ride away. Whenever the military history of those dark days of late May and early June of 1940 is recounted, the stories of Boulogne and Calais will be inextricably linked, for the decision to save the British troops in one of those ports almost certainly led to the sacrifice of those in the other. The story of the battle for Boulogne has many parallels with the story of the battle for Calais but the parallels start long before May 1940.

Both are ancient and important ports and both are steeped in history. Boulogne, like Calais, has played host to some of history's most illustrious figures. It was from the cliff tops near Boulogne that both Julius Caesar and Napoleon Bonaparte looked out with an acquisitive eye across the English Channel towards the coast of England. Both set up large military camps in Boulogne and both developed the port, sheltered from the north by Cap Gris Nez, to assemble a formidable fleet in readiness for an invasion of the British Isles. Caesar succeeded, Napoleon, for various reasons, did not. Nonetheless it is Naploeon's statue, not Julius Caesar's which still looks out towards the English coast from its location just north of the town atop a column more than fifty metres in height.

Just under a century after the French Emperor's final defeat on the fields of Waterloo some of the first units of Sir John French's British Expeditionary Force landed in Boulogne on August 14, 1914, on their

Boulogne at peace. The beach near the Digue Ste. Beuve.

Above and left: **The Port of Boulogne in use by the British during the Great War of 1914-18.**

way to engage the Armies of the Kaiser also on the fields of Belgium. For the next four years Boulogne became the main route for supplies and troop movements into France and one of the main exit ports for the evacuation of wounded. Boulogne like Calais became a bustling British base and tented camps were strung out along the cliff tops between the two ports. At the end of 'the war to end wars' the body of the British Unknown Warrior lay for one night in a Boulogne chapel before it was borne across the Channel to its final resting place amidst English kings in Westminster Abbey.

When war came to this part of France again in May 1940 in the shape of the rampant German panzer divisions of General Heinz Guderian's XIX *Panzerkorps*, the British response to the threat to these two channel ports was remarkably similar. In both cases a brigade consisting of some of the finest troops that Britain could muster were hastily dispatched across the English Channel in an effort to block and secure an ancient port through which the British government might reinforce and re-supply its beleaguered Expeditionary Force in the field.

8

In both cases the garrisons were asked to defend a perimeter far in excess of the strength of the force available. In both cases the troops went into combat against battle hardened German veterans with very little transport, inadequate weaponry – few anti-tank guns, few effective mortars, no mines, no barbed wire – inadequate maps, inadequate communications and inadequate orders which, during peacetime manoeuvres, would have raised gales of laughter from both officers and men. But this was not peacetime and the speed of the German Blitzkrieg had so overwhelmed Allied intelligence sources that the orders simply characterised the chaos and confusion abroad at the highest levels of command.

In Boulogne as in Calais, the initial positions taken up by the British troops were eventually driven in and they were forced to withdraw into the town to face every infantryman's worst nightmare – street fighting in a built up area. In both ports the French garrisons fought heroically during these later urban phases of the fighting, but any attempt at co-ordination on the part of the Allies was sadly lacking in both cases.

That said there was much bravery, real discipline under fire, determination and stoicism on the part of those who took part in the fighting, but the *dénouement* of the story of the battle for Boulogne differed sharply from the story of its northerly neighbour. In the case of Boulogne the British government decided to cut its losses and sent in destroyers to pull its men out before they were engulfed by the advancing German tide. It was this act which, more than any other, condemned the British in Calais to certain death or capture.

The desperate scenes at the harbour of Boulogne as the destroyers engaged machine-gun positions and German vehicles over open sights whilst they evacuated hundreds of men would never be forgotten by those who witnessed it. The British, however, had not consulted the French and their garrison was left to fight on as best it could until it could resist no longer. The French were furious. They felt betrayed and said so. Churchill, who had already decided on the evacuation of Calais 'in principle', now had to choose between saving the men in Calais, as he had saved those in Boulogne, or serving the greater cause of 'Allied solidarity'. He chose the latter course and the decision almost made him physically sick. He later recorded that it was the only time he felt thus during the entire course of a war in which he was to hear many sickening pieces of news.

This then is the story of the battle for Boulogne, the story of a battle which, although short in duration, was an intense struggle against overwhelming odds. It is a story of remarkable discipline amid the utmost confusion, of reckless courage and devotion to duty, of blazing destroyers, of final stands and the bitter taste of captivity told in the words of those who were there.

Jon Cooksey, READING 2002

9

THE PORT OF BOULOGNE

Boulogne is split in two by the considerably altered and widened course of the River Liane as it flows on its way through the port to the English Channel. To the east, within easy walking distance of the busy port, is the Basse Ville, the main shopping and business district gathered around the thoroughfares of the Grand Rue, Rue Faidherbe, Rue Thiers, Rue Victor Hugo and Rue Nationale. Here the visitor will find the majority of hotels, restaurants and shops enclosed in busy one-way streets and pedestrianised precincts. From the Basse Ville the streets rise steeply up towards the Haute Ville, the charming, self contained Old Town, a rough 1,400 metre square of cobbled streets enclosed by the high ramparts, seventeen turrets and four gatehouses of the thirteenth century Citadel. It is largely due to the architectural

The Porte Gayole at the turn of the 20th Century.

An early photograph of the Basilque Notre Dame in the Haute Ville.

importance and beauty of the old town with its magnificent domed Cathedral, the Basilique Notre Dame, that Boulogne has been awarded the title *Ville d'Art et d'Histoire*. The fortifications, along with the chateau, are amongst the best preserved in northern France and a walk along the ramparts offers outstanding views of the town. Beyond the Haute Ville the ground dips before rising up again to the village of St. Martin- Boulogne and the semi-circle of high ground which stretches from Terlincthun in the north to Ostrohove in the south, almost encircling the eastern half of Boulogne. Dominating the town to the east is the long spur of Mont Lambert rising to a height of 189 metres, a formidable and much prized feature for military leaders. Whoever held Mont Lambert would almost certainly hold Boulogne. The line of high ground is easy to follow on the map; the A16 Autoroute scrawls its way across the uppermost slopes following almost exactly the old route known as the Chemin Vert.

To the west of the Liane the flat land by the river is dominated by the industrial zone of fish processing plants, abattoirs and other industry but here, too, the ground rises to the south-west, although not as steeply as that in the east, up to the residential village of Outreau and beyond to Le Portel on the coast. Beyond Outreau to the south the ground rises to what, in winter, is a windswept spur of open fields, before it undulates on its way to a final steep drop at the Channel coast. On the map the shape of the town does not appear to have changed much over sixty years due to the limitations placed upon its growth by the local topography. The town has grown and new housing has pushed its way up the surrounding hills but lines and contours on a map cannot show the pace and development that has taken place

On the ramparts of the Citadel at La Tour Françoise overlooking the valley of the River Liane to the south.

during the last six decades.

The Boulogne battlefields of today are unlike many of those of the First World War. There are no remains of trenches, gaping mine craters or shell holes here; no vast cemeteries like that at Tyne Cot in the Ypres Salient. Boulogne is the foremost fishing port and fish processing centre in France; it is a thriving industrial town with an agricultural hinterland responding to the changing needs of internal and external markets. Much has changed, even during the last few years, not least in terms of the infrastructure of the town and its surroundings. The siting of the Channel Tunnel terminal at Coquelles just to the south east of Calais and the ever increasing volume of cross-Channel traffic into that port since the closure of the ferry service to Boulogne, have been the prime factors in the extensive development of the motorway network in this part of the Pas de Calais.

The A16 Autoroute, opened in 1998, conveys travellers swiftly from Calais before swinging them around that arc of high ground which overlooks Boulogne from the east and over vertiginous viaducts on their journey towards Abbeville, Amiens and the Paris Basin.

The closure of a cross-Channel ferry service with Britain obviously posed a problem for Boulogne in terms of declining tourist revenue, but the opening of the Channel Tunnel and the extension of the A16 motorway provided other possibilities. In anticipation of the closure of the cross-Channel ferry link Boulogne secured the siting of Nausicaa, the French National Centre for the Study of the Sea, on the north-east jetty of the Avant Port. This visitor attraction, the foremost centre for marine study in France, if not northern Europe, brings more than 800,000 people to Boulogne each year. To service their needs and encourage them to explore the town and region further, there are hundreds of hotel rooms and scores of brasseries and restaurants to suit every taste and pocket. In addition to building new roads, other construction work has seen a rash of new industrial and commercial zones spring up to the south near the River Liane and east to utilise and service the passing motorway traffic. It is a town looking to the future with confidence.

For the visitor interested in the battles of 1940, however, many of the developments of the last decade have also swept away a good deal of what remained of the physical evidence of the fighting at key sites. There is little in the immediate vicinity of the Gare Maritime for example, scene of desperate fighting on Friday 24 and Saturday 25 May 1940, as a small mixed force of Welsh guardsmen and French infantry under the command of Major J C Windsor-Lewis of 2 Welsh Guards made their final stand after most of their comrades had been evacuated. If the imagination is allowed a little freedom, however, it is still possible to stand at the Gare Maritime and various other points in and beyond the town and reflect on what it must have been like for those involved in the battle for Boulogne. Although much of the area around the port was destroyed by Allied bombing in raids after the occupation and up to the liberation in 1944, it is still possible to find and explore certain features and fortifications which held particular significance for the British and French defenders and their German assailants.

A Note on Using the Guide and Advice for Visitors

I would venture that it is essential to understand the 'now' in the context of a guidebook if one thinks of the tremendous pace of change in Boulogne during recent years! It is all too easy to neglect unknowingly the site of some action due to the accumulated developments of more than half a century. I know, I have done it and have had to retrace my steps more carefully at a later date.

Personally I have always found it is essential to get out on to the ground and follow in the footsteps or tracks of those who made history here, hoping to increase my knowledge of what happened and why, to make connections and to try to understand. Certainly in the Haute Ville and the port area there is no great need to do anything other than walk. With a battlefield such as Boulogne, however, with quite long distances involved in visiting sites on the outer perimeter – the initial positions of 20 Guards Brigade involved a deployment along a front of almost twelve kilometres for example – it is essential to have some form of transport to get from one site to another. Experienced cyclists should not find the distances involved too taxing, but for most of us the means of transport will be a private car or mini-bus.

In preparing this guide I have assumed that many readers will at some point want to get onto the ground and walk and suggested routes can be found towards the end of the book.

For those who wish to walk I can do no better than reiterate the excellent advice to be found in other guide books in the *Battleground Europe* series, adding only that the application of a good deal of common sense should always be a guiding principle. In Boulogne itself you are never very far from a drink or bite to eat at any one of the many bars and restaurants or shops which line the streets in the lower or upper towns to the east of the River Liane. Neither is it necessary to take any special precautions other than those which require you to dress according to the weather conditions. Depending on your pace or interest, some of the tours may take several hours to complete and pounding the ground, whatever the weather, can be exhausting so strong shoes or a pair of the lighter, 'urban' walking boots are a good idea. In the summer it is a good idea to carry sun cream, a hat and something to drink with you.

Other tours take the visitor out into the countryside along footpaths, roads and tracks and through villages where there is little by way of food and drink so it is advisable to pack enough food and drink to last several hours. Again in summer it is wise to take sensible precautions to avoid excessive exposure to the sun in areas which offer little shade. Those hay fever sufferers amongst us should be well prepared with their medication. It is advisable, in any case, to pack a first aid kit, complete with sting relief. There is nothing worse than being bitten early on in a walk in the country and spending the next three hours scratching your legs rather than enjoying the tour. In winter, waterproof walking boots or Wellingtons are ideal for tramping through mud or wet grass and a spare set of socks may well come in handy.

A good quality map case which hangs around the neck leaving hands free to use a compass or a camera or to jot notes down in a notebook, is a very practical addition to the equipment list. It will ensure that your papers are kept clean and dry for the most part. (See **A Note on Maps** opposite) I have always found that a small pencil case with a selection of pens, pencils and highlighters is a useful item of 'kit' in order to mark up interesting locations or your own variations to routes. A dictaphone is also a boon to enthusiasts who may wish to record their visit in more detail than they would normally be able to do with pen and paper. In that case spare tapes are a must as are spare films for the camera. A medium sized rucksack or 'daysack' will enable you to carry everything on your back comfortably.

A Note on Maps

As well as the maps to be found in the guide, professionally prepared present day maps of the area are essential items. In my view one can never have too many maps but at the very least one should carry the French Institut Geographique National (IGN) map depicting the whole of the area plus another street map of the town. The list below identifies those which I have found most useful:

1) IGN Serie Bleue (Blue Series) entitled *Boulogne-Sur-Mer*, (2104 ET) 'Top 25'. Scale 1:25 000 (1cm = 250 m). The IGN performs almost the same function as our Ordnance Survey. This map covers the whole of the designated area in great detail and includes contours and other topographical features. If you were only to buy one map then this would be it. Fortunately the map is also one of IGN's 'Top 25' series which covers the coastline, forests and mountain regions of France and includes a wealth of additional tourist information which does not appear on most other Blue Series maps.

2) IGN Thematic France Series entitled *Forts & Citadelles, Musees Militaires* (907). Scale 1:1000 000 (1cm = 10km). Covers the military architecture of the whole of France from Vauban to Maginot and shows the location of all the major fortifications and military museums with some interesting information on the reverse.

A free IGNcatalogue is available from their British distributor, World Leisure Marketing and Map World (tel: 01332 343 332 fax: 01332 340 464) or from Hereford Map Centre (tel: 01432 266322 fax: 01432 341874, e-mail: mapped@globalnet.co.uk. The IGN has its own web site at http://www.ign.fr

German tank commander plans his route.

3) Commonwealth War Graves Commission (CWGC) entitled *Calais Lille Bruxelles*. This is the Michelin Map (51), Scale 1:200 000 (1cm = 2km) overprinted with the locations of Commonwealth war cemeteries and memorials. A detailed alphabetical index is also provided. Available from the CWGC (tel: 01628 634221 fax: 01628 771208) The CWGC has an excellent web site at http://www.cwgc.org (e-mail: cwgc@dial.pipex.com) with a page dedicated to its publications.

4) Plan Guide Blay Foldex entitled *Boulogne-s-Mer et Environs*. Approximate scale 1: 9 100 (1cm = 91m) This is

15

a useful street map of the town with a more detailed map of the area around the Haute Ville on the reverse. The map shows almost the whole of the line of the outer perimeter held by 2 Welsh Guards except for a few hundred metres at the very eastern extremities of their line beyond St. Martin-Boulogne. Rather more annoying is that it does not, however, show the more southerly limits of the perimeter held by 2 Irish Guards to the south-east of the village of Outreau. Nevertheless it is worth purchasing for the information it provides on street names. Some useful addresses and telephone numbers are printed on the reverse along with additional tourist information in English. Obtainable from the bookshop on the Grand Rue just below Place Dalton or from Blay Foldex 40-48 Rue des Meuniers, F-93108, Montreuil, Cedex, France. (tel: 149 88 92 10)

It is also worth bearing in mind that many companies publish free maps of the town of Boulogne as a way of advertising local products or services. These can be picked up from the Boulogne Tourist Office on the Boulevard Gambetta and from a number of shops. Many of these maps are restricted to showing the town itself or almost up to the outer perimeter but each one shows something a little different and in any case they are useful for scribbling on if nothing else. Before we leave the subject, do try to obtain the most recent editions of maps. Sometimes the numbers and routes of some of the footpaths shown on the IGN sheets for example, do not always equate to the actual route on the ground.

Travel suggestions

Whether in town or country it is advisable to observe certain common sense rules and courtesies with regard to safety and the local inhabitants who are busy going about their daily activities and earning a living whilst we are visiting the battlefield. Please park cars with care, particularly on roads and lanes in agricultural areas, and always lock valuables and bags that you do not need out of sight in the boot of the car. Observe any 'propriete privee' and other warning notices and exercise care in and around some of the old fortifications by sticking to marked paths and safe areas as indicated.

With the best will in the world accidents can and do happen, so make sure your tetanus jabs are up to date in case you cut or scratch yourself on a piece of rusty metal. In addition to any personal accident insurance you may arrange privately it is always a good idea to carry form E111 with your travel documents. This form is issued free and is attached to a booklet, obtainable from larger post offices, explaining your entitlement to hospital and medical treatment in France and other EC countries.

One of the most attractive features of the Boulogne battlefield from a visitor's point of view is that it is very accessible. Although a direct ferry service is no longer available it is less than thirty minutes drive from Calais thanks to the completion of the A16 Autoroute from Calais to Abbeville. Depending on the departure point in the UK, it is possible to catch an early morning ferry to Calais and spend the best part of a day in Boulogne before returning to Calais and taking an evening crossing for the journey home. The various three and five day deals offered by the cross-Channel operators are also ideal for visitors to Boulogne and the surrounding area. Whether touring on foot, by cycle or in the car it is wise to make preparations as one would in advance of a visit to any other country on the continent. The possible downside of improved accessibility to Boulogne is the risk of increased familiarity which could trip up the unwary. It is tempting perhaps, and especially so on a day visit, to forgo the usual travel precautions of comprehensive personal and vehicle insurance, but it is wise to ensure that every member of the party and the vehicle is adequately covered. Some of the motoring organisations now offer free breakdown and legal expenses cover for up to seventy-two hours for the cost of a telephone call. It should also be remembered that Third Party cover is a minimum requirement when travelling in France. Green cards are no longer required as evidence of minimum cover as inspection of these documents has been abolished at the frontiers. It is advisable, however, to advise your agent or broker of your intended travel plans to ensure that your cover is extended to apply. The list of 'compulsory' items to be carried by motorists as required by French law is also an essential be it a day trip or a two-week stay. These include your licence and vehicle registration documents, a warning triangle, headlamp beam converters and the visible display of the GB plate. Children under the age of ten are not allowed to travel as front seat passengers in France. Carrying a spare set of bulbs, whilst not compulsory, is highly recommended.

Being a large, modern town Boulogne has abundant services and a wealth of hotels and restaurants to suit every taste and pocket. Even at the furthest extremities of the battlefield you are never more than a few kilometres from the town and this makes the search for accommodation and sustenance relatively easy. With this in mind the guide has been prepared so that everyone can use it to suit his or her own itinerary and budget. There may be those who wish to make the best use of a day trip and focus on just one area of the battlefield, whilst others will wish to explore more of the battlefield in greater depth and at a more leisurely pace.

For the latter group, the following list of hotels, some with restaurants, may provide a useful starting point in the search for accommodation and although I have stayed at and eaten in a number of them, the list should not be seen as either definitive or exhaustive nor should it be implied that it reflects any order of merit. Tastes and requirements differ. It is possible to turn up at a hotel 'on spec' and find a comfortable room but for those travelling in larger groups or with people having special requirements that approach may be too risky. In all cases it is worthwhile checking on whether a hotel meets your specific requirements in terms of facilities, availability and budget before setting out from home, particularly during the height of summer.

The staff of the **Boulogne Office de Tourisme** at **24 Boulevard** Gambetta are very helpful, speak good English and will send a comprehensive list of hotels, camp sites and restaurants on request. They can be contacted on, **Tel: 321 10 88 10, Fax: 321 10 88 11 or via e-mail:** ot.boulogne@wanadoo.fr. To call the Tourist Office or for hotel reservations from the UK dial 00 33, followed by the nine digit number given. (If you come across a ten digit number during your searches dial the 00 33 code from the UK and knock off the first 0 of the French number.)

Hotels in Boulogne:

Metropole ***, 51-53,Rue Thiers, 62200 Boulogne-sur-Mer. Tel: 321 31 54 30 Fax: 321 30 45 72. Situated close to the harbour and shops in the heart of the Bass Ville.

Ibis Vieille Villes **, Rue Porte Neuve, 62200 Boulogne-sur-Mer.

Tel: 321 31 21 01, Fax: 321 31 48 25. One of a series of Ibis hotels in Boulogne directly opposite the Porte Neuve and just outside the thirteenth century ramparts of the Haute Ville. Close to where the Germans first breached the ancient ramparts during the latter stages of the battle.

Ibis Plage **, 170,Boulevard Ste.Beuve 62200 Boulogne-sur-Mer. Tel: 321 32 15 15, Fax: 321 30 47 97. Situated on the front a short walk from the Nausicaa marine centre and the harbour. Ten minutes easy walking to the Bass Ville and numerous restaurants. A 'no nonsense' hotel with a lift in the lobby and ample parking on the kerb outside or in the seafront car park opposite.

Formule 1, Z. I. de l'Inqueterie, Route de St. Omer, St. Martin-Boulogne. Tel: 321 31 26 28, Fax: 321 80 22 55.

Hotel Premiere Classe, Lot du Blanc Pignon, Route de St. Omer, St. Martin-Boulogne. Tel: 321 80 46 46, Fax: 321 31 04 03. These are cheap and cheerful yet clean and tidy, tourist motels situated close to the A16 interchange at St. Martin catering for passing business traffic. They are within two minutes drive of the initial positions on the outer perimeter held by 3 and 4 Companies of 2 Welsh Guards on 22/23 May 1940. No reception as such but you can turn up and get a room automatically, if available, by using a credit card at a 'hole in the wall' in the manner of a bank ATM.

Hotels Beyond Boulogne

Copthorne ***, Avenue Charles de Gaulle, 62231,Coquelles. Tel: 321 46 60 60,Fax: 321 85 76 76 e-mail:Copthorne@copthorne.com. Part of a multi-national chain. Built on the site of the Chateau Pigache position south-east of Calais which was held by the Germans and taken by the Allies in September 1944, and opposite a wooden windmill on the Coquelles Ridge. It is on the route taken by some of the tanks of 3 Royal Tank Regiment (3RTR) part of the Calais garrison, on their way to meet elements of the German 1 Panzer Division near the village of Hames Boucres. (See Cooksey. Jon, *Calais 1940 – A Fight to the Finish*, Leo Cooper, Pen and Sword Books, 2000.)

Hotel Normandy **, Place de Verdun, 62179 Wissant. Tel: 321 35 90 11, Fax: 321 82 19 08. Situated some twenty minutes drive by car north along the D940 coast road from Boulogne it is now run by Didier Davies the latest member of the Davies family to run the hotel. Didier is the son of David Davies who has now retired from the hotel business but still owns and runs the Atlantic Wall Museum housed in the German Battery Todt at Audinghen a little further along the coast. David's father, a Welshman who served with the Royal Welch Fusiliers in World War One, stayed in France and married a French girl and went on to run the Hotel. As a boy David had been one of the last civilians to leave Calais before it fell in 1940, due to his father's British citizenship. He is often in the hotel and has a wealth of knowledge about the history of the region and the German Atlantic Wall defences in particular. Most of the Normandy's twenty-eight rooms offer sea views, and it boasts an excellent restaurant. It has the advantage of providing a seaside retreat after the bustle of Boulogne.

Museums

I have already mentioned some interesting web sites and e-mail addresses and, although not directly related to the battle for Boulogne, I would like to draw readers' attention to the '**39-45 Route**' developed by the Calais Tourist Office. This route brings together eight museums or sites of significant interest related to the Second World War, five of which are within easy striking distance of Boulogne. As opening hours and admission charges are subject to change I would advise contacting the sites direct for up to date information in order to save wasted journeys.

Musee de la Guerre, Calais, Parc St. Pierre 62100 Calais, Tel: 321 34 21 57. Situated in the middle of the Parc St. Pierre, opposite the Hotel de Ville, the Calais War Museum is housed in twenty rooms of the ninety-four metre long 'Mako' bunker built by the Germans as a central telephone exchange and HQ of the Port Commandant during the occupation.

Musee de Mur de l'Atlantique – Batterie Todt, 62179 Audinghen, Cap Gris-Nez, Tel: 321 32 97 33/ 321 82 62 01, Fax: 321 82 19 08. Owned and run by Mr. David Davies, the Museum of the Atlantic Wall is just off the D940 south of Audinghen. It is housed in one of seven bunkers built to protect a 380mm German naval gun and exhibits extend over ten rooms with vehicles and a 280mm K5 railway gun outside.

Historique de la Seconde Guerre Mondiale-Ambleteuse, 62164 Ambleteuse. Tel: 321 87 33 01, Fax: 321 87 35 01. Twenty minutes from Boulogne along the D940 coast road or exit 7 from the A16 motorway. The Second World War Museum is on the right hand side of the road in Ambleteuse when driving in the direction of Calais. Laid out over 800 square metres the exhibits and displays follow a chronological order from the Polish campaign to the Hiroshima bomb. Special features include a street in Paris during the occupation and a video film about the Normandy invasion shown in a '1940s cinema'.

Mimoyeques, 62250 Landrethun-Le-Nord, Tel:321 87 10 34, Fax: 321 83 33 10. Site of the famous 'Canons des Londres', the 'London Guns'. Five bunkers were built each housing five, 150mm guns 130m in length, with the aim of firing directly on London.

V2 Base – The Bunker of Eperleques, 62910 Eperleques, Tel: 321 88 44 22, Fax: 321 88 44 84, web site at www. audomarois-online.com. This huge bunker in the forest of Eperlques was built as the first launch base for the German V2 rocket. Classified as a national historical monument in 1985, a laser CD takes the visitor through the history and technology of the site.

The three other sites which complete the '39-45 Route' are a little further afield. They are the **Musee de la Seconde Guerre Mondiale, 'Message Verlaine' – Tourcoing** near the Belgian border, **The Atlantic Wall Museum** in Ostend and the **Fort de Breendonk** north of Brussels. Not part of the '39-45 Route' but 5km from St. Omer is **La Coupole,** the V2 bunker of Helfaut Wizerne 62504, St. Omer, (Tel: 321 93 07 07, Fax: 321 39 21 45). Uniformed hostesses act as guides for a tour lasting up to two hours which takes in the underground galleries, ascent into the five metre thick concrete dome which protected the V2 launch pad and films or audiovisual presentations in two cinemas each with 100 seats.

Acknowledgements

The completion of a book such as this requires the help, support, advice and guidance of a great many people. First and foremost I owe a tremendous debt of gratitude to the surviving veterans of the battle of Boulogne who all gave freely of their time to talk to me about their experiences or to loan precious photographs, memoirs, maps or other illustrations for publication. Of those who served with British units and fought in Boulogne I received encouragement, help and hospitality from Mr. Arthur Boswell, Mr. Joseph Bryan, Mr. Doug Davies, Mr. Arthur Evans C.B.E., Mr. Peter Hanbury, Sir John Leslie, Mr. Syd Pritchard, Mr. W. G. J. Rhys-Parry, Mr. F. E. Smith, Mr. Cyril Sutton, and Mr. Charles Thompson. I am grateful for permission to quote from the published memoirs of Mr. Arthur Evans and Mr. Peter Hanbury.

I received a great deal of help from the families of men involved in the battle. Sir Beville Stanier Bt., son of Sir Alexander Stanier who led 2 Welsh Guards during the battle for Boulogne, was unfailingly helpful and courteous during the early stages of my research and loaned many valuable family documents. I am grateful to him for permission to quote from his father's published memoirs and lecture notes and for permission to publish hitherto unseen photographs.

From institutions I have received considerable assistance from Mr. Roy Lewis, General Secretary of the Welsh Guards Association, who helped put me in touch with many veterans and Captain Vince McEllin, Assistant Regimental Adjutant at RHQ, Irish Guards who gave permission to publish photographs from their archive. I owe a particular debt of gratitude to Regimental Adjutant Lieutenant Colonel Charles Stephens and Sergeant Morgan at RHQ Welsh Guards who allowed me access to paintings held by the Regiment of the fight of 3 Company, 2 Welsh Guards at Mont Lambert crossroads and the evacuation of 1 and 2 Companies from Boulogne. Without their considerable help it would not have been possible to photograph and reproduce illustrations from these unique pictures.

Members of staff at the Public Records Office have provided help and assistance during my research and it is always a pleasure to visit the reading room at the Imperial War Museum where the welcome is always warm and the assistance efficient. In particular I should like to thank Mr. Roderick Suddaby, Keeper of the Department of Documents, who very kindly let me have sight of several documents pertaining to the naval operations during the evacuation from Boulogne which helped shed new light on this important aspect of the battle. Miss Jo Lancaster and her colleagues at the Sound Archive have been most efficient in helping to trace oral accounts of the battle. At the Commonwealth War Graves Commission staff have again responded promptly to my many communications, as has Frau Martina Caspers of the Bundesarchiv in Koblenz, Germany. In France, M. Jean-Pierre Vilbonnet of the Institut Geographique National provided invaluable assistance as did M. Edmond Fauquez, M. Lucien Vasseur and M. Jérôme Bouly of the Mairie de Saint-Martin-Boulogne, whilst in Belgium Mr. Robert Dehon, one of the prime movers in the project to develop Fort de la Creche as an open air museum, proved to be of great help. I thank them all for their time and patience.

Friends have once again rallied to the cause. Ghislaine Pearce has helped to translate another pile of French documents and again I am indebted to my friend Hugo Stockter in Germany who has undertaken much research and, it has to be said, a great deal of travel on my behalf. Hugo has translated a veritable mountain of German material and that, together with his boundless enthusiasm for the project, his clarity, thoroughness and his knowledge of the German Army of 1940, has once more helped to provide an important balance in terms of the perspectives on the battle for Boulogne. Thank you very much Hugo.

Quotations from Crown Copyright Records deposited in the Public Record Office are reproduced by permission of the Controller of Her Majesty's Stationery Office. Extracts from the papers of Major General J.C. Haydon, Captain G.J.A. Lumsden and Mr. Don Harris held by the Imperial War Museum are reproduced by kind permission of the Trustees and, respectively, the Estate of Miss Malise Haydon, Mrs. Daphne Lumsden and Mr. R. Summers.

Although a great many people have contributed to the book it should be pointed out that any errors or omissions are due entirely to me.

Finally, and most importantly I should like to thank my family. My wife Heather and my five year old daughter Georgia have been a constant source of encouragement as they too managed to juggle work and school around my 'disappearances' for hours, or, in some cases, days on end. For their continued understanding and support I am very grateful.

CHAPTER ONE

BLITZKRIEG

The German Blitzkrieg in the west, which exploded forward from positions on the Luxembourg frontier on 10 May 1940, is well documented. Responding to the codeword *Gelb* (Yellow), issued around midday on 9 May the German forces began their astonishing advance across the frontiers of the Netherlands and Belgium towards the French border at 5.35 am the following morning. 'Plan Yellow' decreed that the *schwerpunkt*, the centre of gravity of the attack, would be concentrated in Army Group 'A' on the southern flank which had been allotted seven out of the ten panzer divisions then in existence. These were part of the *Sichelschnitt*, the 'Scythe Stroke', a sweeping drive through the Low Countries and France which had the encirclement and complete annihilation of the Allied armies to the north as its objective. At the southernmost tip of the scythe were the battle proven troops of General Heinz Guderian's XIX Panzer *Korps*.

At the age of fifty-two, Guderian was an audacious leader, brimming with a self-belief which often led him to disregard and exceed the orders of his superiors. He was the 'father' of Germany's panzers, his theoretical work on the use of massed tank divisions, spurred on by other forward thinkers such as Britain's Captain Basil Liddell-Hart among others, led to his promotion to command Germany's first Armoured Corps in 1938. He was a master tactician in armoured warfare and had imbued his divisional commanders with his doctrine of co-ordinated assaults characterised by speed and mobility.

General Guderian

'I had full confidence in my three divisional commanders; they knew my way of fighting and knew that when the Panzers started on a journey they had a ticket to the terminus. For us the objective was the sea. This was obvious!' And that is just what they did. It took just ten days for the first of the panzers to reach the sea: the glory of being the first to reach the coast going to the 2 Panzer Division. They had crossed the old Great War killing grounds in a

SS troops discuss the developing situation with their comrades of a *wehrmacht* panzer unit.

Panzer by the sea. Although not directly involved in the battle for Boulogne, elements of Rommel's 7 Panzer Division, reached their 'terminus', at les Petites-Dallas, on 10 June 1940.

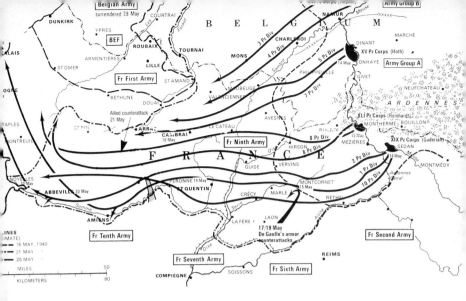

matter of hours and by 7.00 pm on 20 May they had seized Abbeville; the sea almost in sight. Tentatively one tank battalion, the Spitta Battalion, named after its commanding officer, was sent out and reached the sea at Noyelles as dusk closed in. With unconcealed joy the tank crews, who had crossed the Meuse scarcely a week earlier and had covered more than 250 miles in their cramped cockpits, jumped out and filled their lungs with the bracing sea air and drank in the sight of the waves. They had reached the 'terminus'.

The German armour had cut a great swathe through the Allied forces and had created an extended 'Panzer Corridor' which had cut vital road and rail communications between the Allied forces to the north and south. As the men of 2 Panzer celebrated their achievements and paused for breath whilst they awaited further orders they wondered where their next ticket take them.

Guderian was eager to press on but his orders were slow in coming. By the time the German Army had issued its communique declaring, 'Our forces have reached the sea' on the morning of 21 May, Guderian was ready to go. Word had come through towards the end of the previous day that he was to turn north and he had begun to earmark his divisions for the tasks ahead of them. 1 Panzer was to capture Calais whilst 10 Panzer was to advance towards the line of the Aa and push on to seize Dunkirk. 2 Panzer's objective was the capture of Boulogne. Events at Arras on 21 May were, however, to alter Guderian's plans for an early resumption of the attack and ultimately delayed his assault on the Channel Ports. He was later to view the 21 May as a day wasted and an opportunity squandered. The problem was that the British had counter-attacked at Arras with

25

A Horch staff car containing Luftwaffe personnel passes a knocked out British Matilda, two-man tank, near Arras, the scene of ferocious fighting during the Great War.

seventy-four tanks and the 6th and 8th Battalions of the Durham Light Infantry, supported by a force from a single French light armoured division.

The Allied attack was not in itself a huge success, but it had succeeded in. striking a telling blow against the extended northern flank of the 'Panzer Corridor'. Guderian's advance had been so swift and decisive that a precarious gap had developed between the armoured and motorised units in the van of the assault and the supporting infantry following on foot, often two days' march behind. The largely British effort at Arras was proof to Hitler and the German command that the flanks were vulnerable. It had been enough to convince them that Guderian should be made to apply his foot to the brakes, albeit temporarily.

As a result, 10 Panzer was withdrawn from Guderian's command at 6.00 am on 22 May into Group reserve at Doullens. Guderian was furious. Shorn of a third of his force and feeling somewhat cheated in his grand design to take Dunkirk, Guderian decided to use his remaining two divisions in an advance up the coast to capture Boulogne and Calais. At midday Guderian jumped the gun and ordered 2 Panzer to drive up the N1 towards Montreuil via the line Baincthun-Samer and thence to Boulogne without waiting for orders from General Ewald von Kleist, commander of Gruppe von Kleist, his immediate superior. 1 Panzer were to track their path some five miles inland to provide protection for their eastern flank against attack from Calais. In his opinion he had already wasted five hours with his armour standing inactive on the line of the River Canche. As the afternoon wore on and 2 Panzer came within site of Boulogne, Guderian received the welcome news that von Kleist had restored 10 Panzer to his command. Guderian, realising that the prize of Dunkirk and the encirclement of

General Heinz Guderian in his command vehicle during the drive through France. Panzer radio operators decipher a message received on the Enigma encoding machine.

A *Panzerkampfwagen* MkIII of 2 Panzer Division during the advance through France towards Boulogne.

Boulogne and Calais was again a possibility, reacted with characteristic alacrity. Handing the job of taking Calais to 10 Panzer he decided to redirect 1 Panzer eastward, to pass across the southern face of Calais and race on to cross the Aa Canal and thence to Dunkirk. Dunkirk was the prize. That was where the bulk of the Allied force in the north was heading, a force which included the greater part of the BEF. If Dunkirk were to be taken then the Allied forces to the north of the 'Panzer Corridor' would be beaten. The capture of Boulogne and Calais, were not his priority. If the Dunkirk domino fell and the panzers succeeded in isolating any forces which could be landed at the two remaining Channel ports, then sooner or later Calais and Boulogne would tumble.

Five hours later than he had wished, Guderian's tanks of 2 and 10 Panzer Divisions began their advance up the coast towards Boulogne and Calais respectively to winkle out and mop up the defenders of those ancient ports. In Boulogne the two battalions of Guards the 2 Irish Guards and 2 Welsh Guards had sailed in that very morning to bolster the French defence. Those five precious hours gave them a breathing space, albeit brief, in which to organise, take up their positions and wait for the Germans. Five hours was not long but it was better than nothing and the Guards had the German commanders to thank for it.

CHAPTER TWO

WAR IS BETTER THAN FOXHUNTING

Only a year before the Germans launched their attack on France and the Low Countries, Lieutenant Colonel Sir Alexander Stanier, Bt., MC, the newly appointed commanding officer of 2nd Battalion, Welsh Guards had sat at his desk in Chelsea barracks and had written down the strength of his new command. He had come up with a total roll numbering just three men and that included himself. The new battalion had been formed on 18 May and Lieutenant Colonel Stanier had been recalled from service as second in command of 1st Battalion Welsh Guards then in Gibraltar, with orders to build up the new battalion from scratch. Little did he know that he would have exactly one year to build and train his battalion before leading it into battle at Boulogne in May 1940.

'The battalion staff came principally from the first battalion in Gibraltar and some from other establishments in England, with a few transferring in from other regiments. One or two squads of recruits soon joined us from the Guards Depot and eventually we had our first battalion parade in mid-June. From then on we were calling up reservists to train them in the 'new' weapons – the Bren gun, the 2-inch mortar and the anti-tank rifle. Gradually we built up our strength till we had to move out of Chelsea and went in August to the Tower of London where our numbers had reached close on 400 and we took over public duties there. We were at the Tower when war was declared on 3 September.' Lieutenant Colonel Sir Alexander Stanier Bt., MC. CO 2 Welsh Guards[1]

Officers, Warrant Officers and NCOs, 2nd Battalion Welsh Guards on its formation in June 1939. Three in civvies left to right: Captain and Adjutant Robin Rose-Price, Lieutenant Colonel Sir Alexander Stanier Bt., MC, Lieutenant and QM William Bray DCM, MM. Courtesy Sir Beville Stanier Bt.

1st Battalion Welsh Guards officers prior to leaving for duty in Gibraltar, April 1939. Several officers transferred to 2nd Battalion with Lieutenant Colonel Stanier, pictured front row third from left. Courtesy Sir Beville Stanier Bt.

CO's inspection at Chelsea Barracks, June 1939. Courtesy Sir Beville Stanier Bt.

One of the reserve officers who joined the Battalion at this time was Second Lieutenant Peter Hanbury, a twenty-one year-old Cambridge undergraduate who had been placed in charge of 12 platoon of 4 Company. Hanbury soon found that his company commander was determined to make his raw junior officers take their training seriously.

> 'Jack Higgon was my company commander; Cyril Heber-Percy second in command; Dickie Twining and Eddie Beddingfield the other two platoon commanders. Jack was tough. Going to shoot on the miniature range, I said I was not much of a rifle shot. He said I would not go on leave until I was better than 80 out of 100. He said I must learn to take a Bren gun to bits and reassemble it in the dark, therefore my servant was to draw one of the company Bren guns in the evening and I was to practise in my room with a kit bag over my head until I could do this.' Second Lieutenant Peter Hanbury. OC 12 Platoon, 4 Company, 2 Welsh Guards.[2]

Apart from a short spell at Theydon Bois in Essex the battalion mounted King's Guard and performed other public duties in the capital throughout the autumn and winter of 1939-40. Peter Hanbury was sent to drill his platoon in the moat and his men made the most of his inexperience as a drill instructor, some stopping whilst others marched on or turned on his orders. Just when he felt that his platoon had made a complete fool of him the Adjutant appeared to see how he was getting on and his men drilled perfectly. Hanbury realised for the first time what a superb collection of men his guardsmen were. Much to the chagrin of Lieutenant Colonel Stanier life at the Tower left little time for real infantry training in the field, so he was happy when the battalion was relieved of London duties in April

1940 and ordered to Old Dean Common Camp near Camberley to become part of 20 Guards Brigade commanded by Brigadier Sir Oliver Leese DSO, with 2 Irish Guards and 5 Loyal Regiment.

2 Battalion Irish Guards had been raised two months after 2 Battalion Welsh Guards on 15 July 1939, under the command of Lieutenant Colonel Joseph Charles Haydon who had been Military Assistant to Secretary of State for War Leslie Hore-Belisha until the spring of that year. Like the Welsh the Irish had been stationed in London for the autumn and winter of 1939-40 at Wellington Barracks. There they had kicked their heels whilst awaiting the call to action, taught Canadians to mount King's Guard, marched through London or trained, 'self consciously in St James's or Hyde Park', as Londoners watched on.

A call to reinforce their comrades in 1st Battalion Irish Guards in Norway came in April but was amended two days later. Camberley was substituted for Norway and so on 22 April the Irish Guards moved to the tented camp at Old Dean Common to join 2 Welsh Guards. With little prospect of immediate action Lieutenant Colonel Stanier, aware that nobody had had any leave whatsoever since the outbreak of war, badgered his superiors into approving a week's leave for all ranks over Whitsuntide. Leave parties were also organised for the Irish Guards and the guardsmen looked forward to spending time with their families. With so far to travel, special leave trains for the Irish were due to leave early on 10 May, the Friday before Whit Monday, with the Welsh due to leave the next day but

King's Guard duty at Buckingham Palace during wartime – autumn, winter 1939-1940.

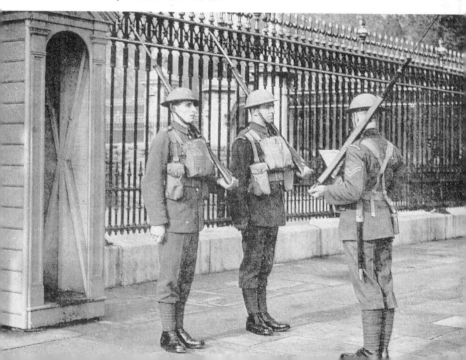

the Germans had other ideas for the Whitsuntide holidays. On the same day the Irish leave parties got away the German Army began its *Blitzkrieg* on the western front. With the full extent of the German attack unclear the Welsh leave parties got away on 11 May. No sooner had they gone than Lieutenant Colonel Stanier received a message informing him that the Germans had invaded Holland and the Low Countries and that 2 Welsh Guards were to sail immediately with 2 Irish Guards forming a small force to assist the Dutch in safeguarding their government and stabilising the situation in The Hague. If the Dutch government left The Hague the Guards had orders to return at once.

By the time the War Office telegram arrived cancelling all leave most of

Lieutenant Colonel Sir Joseph Haydon (centre) and Secretary of State for War, The Rt. Hon. Leslie Hore-Belisha on their way to a cabinet meeting during the Munich crisis of 1938.
Courtesy the Estate of Miss Malise Haydon

Officers of 2nd Battalion Irish Guards. Victoria Barracks, Windsor, September 1939.

Courtesy Sir John Leslie

Guardsman Charles Thompson (right).
Courtesy Mr Charles Thompson

the leave parties were well out of reach. Welsh Guardsman Syd Pritchard had just turned twenty and was well on his way to the Land of His Fathers.

'At the beginning of May they'd sent the battalion on leave and it was cancelled. I'd got as far as Cardiff with a friend when I heard. I was in the Aberdare train actually and I had full intentions of going back, honestly I went back onto the London platform and I met some others who said, "they've some bloody hope we're going home." We hid in the lavatory from Cardiff to Bridgend. My friend went to Swansea to his home, another boy went to the Rhondda and I went to Aberdare! We didn't have telegrams. When we got back to Old Dean Common it was deserted and we were taken to the guardroom and asked why we hadn't come back and we said we never had a telegram. Then the boys came back.' Guardsman Syd Pritchard. 4 Company, 2 Welsh Guards. [3]

Others were not so lucky.

'On leaving London for a period of field training I was recalled suddenly from leave to make up a company to rescue the Dutch Royal Family as the Germans had invaded and it was imperative that we brought them out before they were captured.' Guardsman Charles Thompson. 12 Platoon, 4 Company, 2 Welsh Guards. [4]

It was clear that it would take time for all the men to get back so a composite force was made up of the first men to return. Four companies of Irish Guards augmented by one company of Welsh Guards under the overall command of Lieutenant Colonel Haydon made up what was known as 'Harpoon Force'. They landed at the Hook of Holland at dawn on Whit-Monday, 13 May and re-embarked by the skin of their teeth forty-eight hours later having lost all their kit covering the evacuation of the Dutch Queen Wilhelmina and her government amid a panic of fleeing refugees and heavy German bombing. The Irish lost eleven killed. An officer of the destroyer HMS *Whitshed* later wrote that the Irish Guards contingent

'...marched down the jetty and on board as if they were parading in the forecourt of Buckingham Palace. It was grand to watch them.'

It was the first of three occasions in the space of a month that the *Whitshed* would sail in the company of the Irish Guards.

The men of 'Harpoon Force' marched back into the camp at Old Dean

Guardsman Doug Davies (*right*) Caterham Guards Depot 1939. Douglas Morton, on his right, was one of the first Welsh Guardsmen to lose his life.

Courtesy Mr Doug Davies

Guardsman Syd Pritchard

Courtesy Mr Syd Pritchard

Common through lines of cheering Welsh Guardsmen like Syd Pritchard and Doug Davies of 3 Company who had not returned from leave in time and were now eager to hear hair-raising stories of their comrades' first action. With very few casualties some of the Welsh contingent came back enthusing about their experiences. 'War is better than foxhunting', remarked one of the Welsh officers to Lieutenant Colonel Stanier. Those who had not made the crossing to the Hook need not have felt left out. Britain's new Prime Minister, Winston Churchill, had only been in office for five days and although he was unaware of the finer details of the German advance there was little doubt that the situation of the BEF gave grave cause for concern. With the Germans straddling the Allied lines of communication it was clear that something had to be done to secure the Channel ports of Dunkirk, Calais and Boulogne as a means of supplying the BEF and, heaven forbid, getting them out if the worst came to the worst. Churchill still believed that the situation could be stabilised by taking the fight to the Germans and breaking out southward towards the Somme and in the light of information he had to hand there was no reason to doubt that the Allies could not do so. Unfortunately that information was subject to uncertainty, conjecture and out if date intelligence. Nevertheless a breakout to the south would need support and the Channel ports were vital in keeping the supply lines open. Plans to defend the ports began to be made in a fog of rumour and half-truths. The Guards of 20 Brigade were being pencilled in as part of Churchill's plan. In less than a week those guardsmen who had not made the trip to the Hook of Holland would get their chance in battle and the survivors of that ordeal would have more than enough of their own stories to tell.

1. Lieutenant Colonel Sir Alexander Stanier Bt. MC. OC 2 Welsh Guards. *Sammy's Wars.*
2. Second Lieutenant Peter Hanbury. OC 12 Platoon, 4 Company, 2 Welsh Guards *A Not Very Military Experience.*
3. Guardsman Syd Pritchard. 4 Company, 2 Welsh Guards. Author's Tape Transcript
4. Guardsman Charles Thompson. 12 Platoon, 4 Company, 2 Welsh Guards. Letter to author.

CHAPTER THREE

AN INCONVENIENT AND TIRESOME MOMENT

At around 11.00 am on 21 May 1940 a despatch rider drove up to 2 Irish Guards battalion HQ at Old Dean Common Camp near Camberley with an urgent message for Lieutenant Colonel Haydon. It was the order to move on active service. Colonel Haydon's men had only recently returned from an energetic night exercise with 2 Welsh Guards. They had arrived back at camp tired, dirty and ravenous and after wolfing their breakfasts they had scattered to their tents to sleep. For their CO the order to move 'could not have arrived at a more inconvenient or tiresome moment,' but he was a professional soldier and tiresome or not he determined to get his battalion packed up and ready to move by 'zero' hour at 3.30 pm. Efforts by the brigade staff to postpone the time of departure until 6.00 pm were brushed aside. The War Office were unaware that the men of 20 Brigade had had no sleep, all it knew was that the German Army was moving quickly through France and that the Channel ports were vulnerable. A Territorial battalion

Elements of a German reconnaissance unit moving at speed through the French countryside. Their breathtaking advance had sent the Allies reeling back towards the Channel ports.

of Queen Victoria's Rifles supported by 3 Royal Tank Regiment would sail for Calais the next day followed by 1 Rifle Brigade and 2 King's Royal Rifle Corps on 23 May. Exhausted or not, dirty or not, 20 Guards Brigade were going to Boulogne. Immediately the slumbering peace of the camp was torn asunder by shouts of 'pack up' and 'prepare to move' and the sleepy Irishmen roused themselves, grumbled and got on with their jobs.

Sergeant Arthur Evans
Courtesy Mr Arthur Evans

Sergeant Arthur Evans and the rest of 2 Irish Guards anti-tank platoon were not with them. The anti-tank platoon, commanded by Lieutenant Anthony Eardley-Wilmot, had spent a pleasant week billeted at St. Mary's Bay holiday camp whilst they had test-fired their four new Peugeot 37 mm anti-tank guns on the ranges at Lydd in Kent. Their week over, on May 21 they packed up and started out on the journey to rejoin the battalion.

'Somewhere between Tenterden and Goudhurst the convoy was halted by a despatch rider who handed an envelope to our platoon commander, Lieutenant A R Eardley-Wilmot. The message instructed us to retrace our steps and proceed to Dover for embarkation to France as part of the 20 Guards Brigade...Having familiarised ourselves with our new weapons on the Lydd ranges we rolled along the A259 – four 15cwt trucks each towing a gun and carrying its crew and two, 2-ton trucks with our kit and other supplies. I was driving the leading truck with the Lieutenant beside me. Just outside Folkstone we called in at a roadside café to replenish ourselves. I did not know it then but that was the last good meal I would eat for several years.' Sergeant Arthur Evans, **2 i/c Anti-Tank Platoon, 2 Irish Guards.**[1]

The anti-tank platoon had driven all day in perfect weather, cheered on their way by civilians who had lined the roads 'in this quintessential corner of England.' They reached Dover in the late afternoon and joined other lines of transport heading for the docks. Sergeant Evans handed a letter to a little girl called Sheila and asked her to post it for him. She did and it was the last his parents heard of him for many months. The rest of 2 Irish Guards at the head of the brigade column caught up with the anti-tank platoon on the quayside at Dover at around 9.30 pm. It was almost midnight when 2 Welsh Guards, following on, arrived. They had been delayed due to an air raid warning in Folkestone during which civilians had abandoned their cars and blocked the roads. It turned out to be a false alarm; the target of the *Luftwaffe* being the docks at Calais. Lieutenant

Colonel Stanier had a complete battalion travelling in requisitioned buses apart from his own anti-tank platoon, which had been training at Hythe. The President of the Officers' Mess Committee was away buying stores from Fortnum and Mason in London, delicacies shortly to be abandoned in Boulogne to the delight of the German soldiery.

On reaching Dover the air-raid warning was still in force and Lieutenant Colonel Stanier along with his Adjutant Captain Robin Rose-Price, made their way to the *Lord Warden Hotel* with great difficulty. There he was told for the first time what his battalion's task would be. Brigadier Oliver Leese had been called to Lord Gort's HQ with the BEF in France some two days before and Lieutenant Colonel Stanier's new Brigadier was William 'Billy' Fox-Pitt, an old comrade from 1 Welsh Guards who had been one of the first officers appointed to the regiment on its creation in 1915. They had served together during the latter stages of the First World War when Stanier had been a young subaltern and Fox-Pitt a captain. Fox-Pitt had gone on to command the 1st Battalion from late 1934 to early in 1938. From what he was told Lieutenant Colonel Stanier understood that the brigade were being despatched to Boulogne,

> '...to protect a base. But there was no idea that the Germans were anywhere near and that we would be a reserve for the big counter-attack that we expected to go from Arras or wherever it was going to be.'
>
> **Lieutenant Colonel Sir Alexander Stanier Bt., MC. CO 2 Welsh Guards.**[2]

Brigadier Fox-Pitt told Stanier that he was to get his battalion on board a cross-Channel ferry, the SS *Biarritz*, which was due to sail at two o'clock on the morning of 22 May. Stanier and Rose-Price were faced with the Herculean task of organising the loading of all their men and equipment in less than two hours. The ensuing chaos at the Dover quayside set the tone for all further embarkations of British units crossing the Straits of Dover to defend the Channel ports during the following few days.

Boarding the *Biarritz*, Stanier was amazed by the absence of any member of the crew although troops of the Royal Engineers and dock workers were in abundance.

> 'We found there was no crew on board because of the [air-raid] alert – they had all gone to their shelters. We could see a raid in progress on Calais. The battalion were sent for and ordered to drive up to the quay-side, but the Irish Guards were in front and there was a terrific traffic jam. We had to get the goods unloaded from the transport and have it man-handled to the ship, as we couldn't shift the transport, and we couldn't blame the Irish Guards who were in front, for blocking by their transport. Then the 'all clear' went. The Captain of the ship said we had too many men and too much stuff on board and that we should have to shift some of each. He already had his holds full of equipment that had been taken over once and brought back again. It was thus decided to take off Number 1 Company [Captain Heber-

Officers of 2 Welsh Guards prior to embarkation for Boulogne. Courtesy Sir Beville Stanier Bt

Percy], *and some stores. The signal equipment, which was in panniers, was taken off, as it was easy to move. Another ship was chartered to take this company and other troops across, but it had no steam up. Major Vigor was left to follow with this load.'* **Lieutenant Colonel Sir Alexander Stanier Bt. MC. OC 2 Welsh Guards.[3]**

Several men recalled seeing the holds of the *Biarritz* full of rolls of barbed wire and screw pickets which the French stevedores had refused to unload on the ship's last run to Boulogne early the previous morning. With sixty tons of equipment already aboard it was little wonder that the *Biarritz* was packed solid. Number 1 Company began to unload their equipment to await the arrival of the other ship, the SS *Mona's Star*.

As the men boarded the ship Guardsman Arthur Boswell of 8 Platoon, 3 Company, recalled that every man was handed a tin of 'Machonachie's' stew, a sausage roll and a bar of chocolate. He remembered the incident well as they turned out to be the last army rations he would receive.

Eventually the battalion, less all stores and transport, was ready to embark. The battalion only had essential weapons, ammunition and digging tools with them at the expense of all else. Stanier was told that another ship would follow on and bring the rest of the equipment but not the transport. There would be plenty of transport available in Boulogne he was assured. Shorn of most of his stores, Lieutenant Colonel Stanier's command was now split between two ships, one of which would sail four hours later than the other. It was not an enviable way for any CO to lead his men into their first major battle.

Guardsman Arthur Boswell (left) with his friend Guardsman Frank Jones. Courtesy Mr Arthur Boswell

A short distance up the quay Lieutenant Colonel Haydon of 2 Irish Guards found himself in much the same position as Stanier. After a quick

41

Above: Czech built Pz
Kpfw 38(t)s, belonging
to 7 Panzer Division,
drive towards the
Somme River with
infantry in support.

Right: French civilians
flee before the
onslaught.

Below: Evidence of
Stuka bomb damage
as a German mobile
unit avoids the debris.

meal of stew, bread and tea his men had begun to load their equipment onto the *SS Queen of the Channel* only to find the same cramped conditions. It soon became apparent that it would not accommodate all the men and their equipment and although it was obvious to all on the quayside it took another hour and a half to convince the War Office that another ship was a necessity. As the Welsh Guards had done, the men of Number 1 Company Irish Guards under Captain C R McCausland humped their kit back onto the quay to await the *SS Mona's Star*. McCausland's company would later arrive in position on the outskirts of Boulogne at almost the same moment as the Germans launched their first attack on the front held by the Irish.

Eventually the main body of the force was ready to sail with the breaking dawn on 22 May. The destroyer HMS *Whitshed* led the way followed by the *Queen of the Channel* and then the *Biarritz* with the destroyer HMS *Vimiera* abeam as an additional escort. Before they had set sail the Dover port authorities had received a signal from a trawler lying off Boulogne to the effect that German tanks had been reported two miles south of the town although in reality 2 Panzer Division was not ordered forward from the Abbeville area by Guderian until noon that same day. For some of the men on board, however, the task of loading had revealed how painfully lacking they were in the most basic weapons of modern warfare. They had no wire, no anti-tank mines, no grenades and no 3-inch mortars. The signalling kit had been removed from the ships as it had been easy to carry. Although Lieutenant Colonel Haydon was of the opinion that a battalion without its own transport lost about fifty per cent of its fighting efficiency. Neither the Irish nor the Welsh had any apart from a few motorcycles and carriers now parked on the upper decks of the *Queen of the Channel*. Small arms ammunition and picks and shovels would not hold German tanks for long. The great hope was that both battalions could pick up some of these essential supplies on the dockside at Boulogne. One ray of hope was that the brigade anti-tank platoon of four Peugeot 37mm anti-tank guns, under Lieutenant Eardley-Wilmot and Sergeant Arthur Evans, was safely on board the destroyer *Whitshed* along with Brigadier Fox-Pitt and brigade HQ. It was true that the brigade had no wire, mines or mortars and had not been allowed to load its own transport, but one item of

**Brigadier
William Fox-Pitt**

'essential' equipment to counter the panzer threat now nestling in the hold of the *Whitshed* would doubtless have chilled the heart of any German soldier had he known of its presence on board. It was a box of white military umpires' arm-bands!

For the second time in a little over a week Guardsman Charles Thompson was sailing out of Dover,

> '...a port that I had left a short time ago for Holland. I was nineteen years old and so much had happened in the past year, here I was on another adventure which was to prove more than I appreciated at the time even though I had the experience of Holland behind me, of having been dive-bombed by a screaming German plane with machine-guns blazing before dropping its bombs and also other actions to be expected in war. I watched the white cliffs fade into the distance, wondering once more if I would see them again.' Guardsman Charles Thompson. 12 platoon, 4 Company, 2 Welsh Guards.[4]

1. Sergeant Arthur Evans, 2 i/c Anti-Tank Platoon, 2 Irish Guards. *Sojourn in Silesia*
2. Lieutenant Colonel Sir Alexander Stanier Bt., MC. CO 2 Welsh Guards. *Gort's Army -The British Expeditionary Force of 1939-1940.* IWM Sound Archive - 7175/7
3. Lieutenant Colonel Sir Alexander Stanier Bt., MC. CO 2 Welsh Guards. Lecture Notes 1945 in the possession of Sir Beville Stanier Bt.
4. Guardsman Charles Thompson. 12 Platoon, 4 Company, 2 Welsh Guards. Letter to author.

As 20 Brigade sails for France the German armour continues its westward drive. Here French colonial troops are caught on camera surrendering to elements of a German panzer division.

CHAPTER FOUR

WHEN YOU'VE KILLED TWELVE GERMANS YOU CAN COME BACK HOME

With the Channel calm the crossing to Boulogne was uneventful. As the convoy neared Boulogne the *Whitshed* carrying Brigadier Fox-Pitt steamed ahead to get in touch with the Adjutant General, Lieutenant General Douglas Brownrigg, in command of Rear Headquarters BEF based in Wimereux, a coastal resort four kilometres north of Boulogne. On board the *Biarritz* Guardsman Doug Davies of Number 3 Company 2 Welsh Guards, led by the fearless and hugely respected Major J C Windsor-Lewis of Aberdare, was issued with a cloth bandolier containing fifty rounds of small arms ammunition. That was all he was to carry into battle. Guardsman Syd Pritchard of 4 Company had already received his issue of fifty rounds on the bus whilst travelling to Dover. During a stop for sandwiches a cheery RSM Grant had told the men, 'this is your issue. When you've killed twelve Germans you can come back home'.

Major J C Windsor-Lewis.

As the rest of the convoy neared its destination many of the guardsmen saw their first glimpse of war. The 6,477 ton French oil tanker *Ophelie* was

The pall of black smoke from the striken tanker *Ophelie* is clearly visible from the heights near the village of St. Martin.

Courtesy Mairie de Saint-Martin-Boulogne

still ablaze after being bombed three kilometres off the coast during the night of 20-21 May. She was an eerie sight in the half-light of dawn, the flames spreading a deep red glow under the billowing pall of thick black smoke.

'My mate was a seafaring boy. He'd been brought up near the sea his father was a lighthouse keeper on the Mumbles so we got together on the boat and he looked after me. I remember "Jeff" [Guardsman Bert Jeffers] *and me were priming hand grenades and I felt so sick and he said "I'll take you upstairs." When we got upstairs the first thing we saw was a tanker going up in flames. That cured my seasickness.'* Guardsman Syd Pritchard. 11 Platoon, 4 Company, 2 Welsh Guards.[1]

'Approaching Boulogne at dawn, it was startlingly obvious that the Stukas had had a field day. The docks, warehouses and buildings surrounding the harbour were in ruins and still smoking. CSM McGarrity, in whose company I had served in Cairo before the war turned to me with a foreboding expression and said "We will never get out of here." His pessimistic attitude surprised me. Firstly he was supposed to exude leadership and enhance morale. Secondly, until then I had been under the naïve impression that we were on our way to Berlin!' Sergeant Arthur Evans, 2 i/c Anti-Tank Platoon, 2 Irish Guards.[2]

Rain began to fall as the ships reached the mouth of the port where the boom was opened and the convoy entered the narrow harbour. The *Biarritz* eventually came alongside at exactly the spot where Lieutenant Colonel Stanier had landed in France as a nineteen year-old ensign in 1918 on his way to join 1 Welsh Guards in the trenches near Arras.

'The quayside was absolutely crowded with people. Lines of communication, the Adjutant General's staff, everybody coming from rear headquarters being evacuated to England whilst the rest of the Army was going to Dunkirk. The Duke of Gloucester's two chargers for instance I remember standing there with their groom who asked me whether I could help him get them on board. They were all those sort of people... just standing there... no barging or shoving about.' Lieutenant Colonel Sir Alexander Stanier Bt., MC. CO 2 Welsh Guards.[3]

Lieutenant General Brownrigg had orders to evacuate what were rather unflatteringly called 'useless mouths'; non-combatant troops who would eat into scarce resources if allowed to stay in the theatre of operations. These men it seemed were acting under orders. There were even gardeners of the Imperial War Graves Commission who had tended the British First World War cemeteries in the area and were now ready to be evacuated with their families. These civilians with British passports had been separated from the rest of the refugees and collected together by men of 657 General Construction Company Royal Engineers under command of Captain F A Rayfield, who witnessed their departure aboard HMS *Whitshed*. That said, further along the quay there was considerable confusion as disorganised groups of wounded and able-bodied French, Belgian, Dutch and British soldiers mixed with civilian refugees and even a few German prisoners, scrambled for places aboard the newly arrived cross-Channel steamers. The scene which greeted the Irish, as they lined the decks of the *Queen of the Channel*, was not heartening. Fitzgerald's *The History of the Irish Guards in the Second World War* records that the quay was a scene of 'squalid confusion.'

'It looked as if thousands of suitcases had been emptied on the ground by manic customs officers, and trampling over this sodden mass of clothes, bedding and filthy refuse was a horde of panic-stricken refugees and stray soldiers waiting to rush the ships. The battalion could not even disembark 'til sailors and Guardsmen with fixed bayonets had cleared a lane through the sorry mob. The tide was low, none of the cranes were working and refugees, with the ingenuity of despair, found endless ways to board the ship – everything conspired to delay the unloading.'

Whilst the two commanding officers went off in search of Brigadier 'Billy' to find out what they were supposed to do, the battalions began the laborious process of disembarkation and assembly in the customs sheds on the dockside. During unloading Lieutenant Peter Hanbury witnessed a morale sapping sight.

'Hell of a shambles in which Eddie [Beddingfield] *and I remained on board, while Dickie* [Twining] *and Jack* [Higgon] *organised the shore side.*

Men of 2 Irish Guards unloading boxes of biscuits from the *Queen of the Channel* onto the Quai Chanzy in Boulogne during the morning 22 May 1940. Courtesy RHQ Irish Guards

Looking south along the Quai Chanzy where Irish Guards are unloading stores from the *Queen of the Channel*.

Men of 2 Irish Guards prepare to move off from the quayside to march out to their positions in the village of Outreau. Courtesy RHQ Irish Guards

The cranes and the French had given up work so everything had to be manhandled. Eventually before we were half unloaded the RAMC rushed on. It was extremely upsetting to have the ship blocked, so that it was impossible to walk along the gangways, and it also shook one's morale to see 400 men all wounded and a few dead before the battle started. Eddie and I worked at the beginning of a chain unloading stores in the hold until we nearly dropped, and at that moment an air raid came and we leapt off the ship as she set off to get out of port.' Second Lieutenant Peter Hanbury. OC 12 Platoon, 4 Company, 2 Welsh Guards.[4]

Guardsman Arthur Boswell managed a brief exchange with one of the wounded men waiting to embark for England. 'What's it like up there?' he asked, 'You'll find out,' came the laconic reply. At the time Arthur Boswell was labouring under the impression that 'the front' was a 'couple of hundred miles away!' As the Guards came off the ships they trooped into the customs sheds on the quayside where they fretted with impatience awaiting the return of their commanding officers. Sergeant Arthur Evans suddenly heard a gunshot from the direction of the Welsh contingent. The word went round that a Welshman had shot himself in the foot but the man, another by the name of Davies, was in Lieutenant Hanbury's platoon and he had witnessed the incident.

'On the shore Davies blew his thumb off, and I was very nearly sick. He suffered frightfully, poor boy. Sgt. Richardson was very efficient in putting on a first aid dressing. Sergeant Gould was sick – that made me feel much better to know that other people felt worse than me.' Second Lieutenant Peter Hanbury. OC 12 Platoon, 4 Company, 2 Welsh Guards.[5]

It was sometime around 11.00 am when the two ships began to leave with their cargo of wounded and non-combatants but by that time Lieutenant Colonels Stanier and Haydon had returned from their briefing with Brigadier Fox-Pitt and were moving forward to make a detailed reconnaissance of their allotted positions.

The Brigadier had met Lieutenant General Brownrigg at his HQ in Wimereux at 7.00 am that morning and had been told that according to reports received one German motor transport column had been reported at Etaples 26 kilometres down the coast with tanks in the area of the Forest of Crécy. To combat this threat Brownrigg told Fox-Pitt that the dispositions of British troops beyond the boundaries of Boulogne were thought to amount to a few road blocks held by a handful of Royal Engineers and anti-aircraft personnel sited between twelve and fourteen kilometres out of Boulogne along the main roads leading south and south-east. In the town itself there were estimated to be over 1,500 British personnel belonging to the Auxiliary Military Pioneer Corps (AMPC) whom, according to the official report later compiled by 20 Guards Brigade,

'...had not taken up any tactical positions, and were of no military

value, as the officers and NCO's had no control over them, and it was found impossible to form them into a fighting force.'

These troops were in addition to the anti-aircraft defence for Boulogne which consisted of eight 3.7 inch guns of 2 Heavy Anti-Aircraft Regiment, eight machine guns of 58 Light Anti-Aircraft Regiment and one battery of 2 Searchlight Regiment.

The observation that the AMPC were of 'no military value' was perhaps a little harsh under the circumstances despite the fact that its ranks were filled with a medley of non-military skilled volunteer workers, young conscripts and middle aged and 'elderly' reservists, ten thousand of whom had been recalled to the 'Colours' in September 1939. It was true that in the early days of the war the AMPC companies in France had earned an unenviable reputation as unkempt, ill-disciplined bodies of men, lacking in military training and with perhaps only one in five armed and able to use their obsolete rifles. Morale had been poor, *esprit de corps* non-existent; the reservists clung to their old regimental ties and saw their drafting to the 'inferior' AMPC as a slight. It was not an uncommon sight in those early days for up to one hundred men to be brought up to their respective

orderly rooms each morning for some breach of discipline or regulations. However, their elderly senior officers were almost wholly men with long military records and although units of command were large – three officers to more than two hundred men – slowly but surely they began to improve both discipline and the woeful lack of supplies from the higher authorities. One such man was Colonel Donald Dean commanding 5 Group AMPC. If the men of 5 Group could not look up to Dean then they could not look up to anyone for Dean was entitled to wear the ribbon of the Victoria Cross (VC) on his breast, Britain's most esteemed military decoration earned for valour and leadership whilst holding a precarious position north-west of Lens under heavy fire between 24-26 September 1918.

Colonel Donald Dean VC

On 19 May Dean's 5 Group was in Doullens and, with the Germans sweeping around the Allies to the south, he was ordered to get his command to Boulogne by whatever means possible. Between 10 and 18 May he had managed to put Doullens in a state of defence and had scrounged enough rifles to arm half of his men by the time his 1,200 strong command set off on the twenty-seven kilometre journey to St. Pol which they reached that night. Throughout the following day Dean had, by bribery and persuasion, encouraged a train driver to take his men to Boulogne. After a small party had been despatched to the south-

Battle map of 10 Panzer Division showing their advance towards Calais. The capture of Boulogne was assigned to 2 Panzer Division

Courtesy Bundesarchiv Freiburg

10. Schtz. Brig.
S.R. 86
I./S.R. 69
1./A.R. 90
1.Kp. Pi 49
1.Kc. Pz. Jg. L-A
1.Battr. Fla 71

S.R
I./A
1 Kp
1 Ba
1 Kp

Franzosen
450 Mann

Marsch de

S.R. 86
II./S.R. 86
1./A.R. 90
Pz. Jg. 251

Div. Stab
Stab 10. Schtz. Brig.
S.R. 69
I./S.R. 86
A.R. 90 m. I/A.R 105

east to engage motor cycle reconnaissance units of 6 Panzer Division near Nuncq, the Pioneers had left that evening and arrived in Wimereux on the morning of 21 May having collected small parties from an assortment of other AMPC companies and retiring units such as 5 Buffs. Dean's command had by then swelled to 1,500. General Brownrigg had immediately ordered Dean to guard his HQ and early on 22 May issued a further order for him to lead a party of 250 men to hold the crossings of the Canche between Etaples and Montreuil. Dean had set off but soon realised he had been outflanked by the Germans and withdrew to Boulogne just in time to witness the arrival of 20 Brigade. As befits a holder of the VC he had reported to Fox-Pitt and put his men at the Brigadier's disposal. Some of these men, experienced old soldiers, would, despite their reputation and the reservations of the regular Army officers, play their part in the coming battle.

As far as the French were concerned, three battalions of their 21 Infantry Division, led by General Lanquetot, were thought to have thrown a protective arm around the south and south-east of the town on a line from Neufchâtel to Samer, about fourteen kilometres away, with the intention of extending the line as far as Desvres when the rest of the division arrived by train from the east. In fact there were not three full battalions at all. The division had been on the move from the Hazebrouck area since 12 May on their way to Abbeville to help stiffen the Somme line. On 20 May General Lanquetot had made ready to follow his motorised units but on reaching St. Omer he had been informed that the Germans had seized the Somme crossings. He had headed for Boulogne the next day and at 6.00 pm on 21 May had been ordered to defend Boulogne with whatever troops he had

French troops advance to block the lightning German advance.

available. The only units of his own division which had not managed to cross the Somme before the Germans took the bridges were four 25 mm guns of the 48 Infantry Regiment near Neufchâtel, and 1 and 3 Battalions of 65 Infantry Regiment with one battery of 75s around Questrecques near Desvres. Troops from a divisional instruction centre were pressed into service to support these units near the town of Samer. In addition Lanquetot could call on a number of French naval gunners who manned five coastal batteries, the guns of which could only fire seaward.

One such battery was Fort de la Creche, built in the late nineteenth century on high ground overlooking the town two kilometres to the north, and held by a detachment of French naval gunners under *Lieutenant de Vaisseau* de Forton, with one troop of British 2 Heavy Anti-Aircraft Regiment armed with 3.7 inch guns in close proximity. There were also up to 2,000 French recruits in the Old Town or Haute Ville area who were deemed unready for combat by their superiors and almost 4,000 raw Belgian recruits, many unarmed, aged between sixteen and twenty-one who had been evacuated from Etaples and whose commander wished them to be removed to England post haste.

Brownrigg's instructions to Fox-Pitt were simple, 'Boulogne was to be held'. The Brigadier was also told that a battalion of tanks and a battalion of the Queen Victoria's Rifles were due to land that night at Calais and that he could expect them the next morning to bolster his defence. With that Fox-Pitt was issued with just five one-inch maps of the area for the whole brigade and a few of smaller scale before making his way back to the harbour in Boulogne to brief his battalion commanders. Brigadier Fox-Pitt then set out to reconnoitre the town and its environs in the company of Lieutenant Colonel Haydon and the commanding officer of 275 Anti-Tank Battery of 69 Anti-Tank Regiment.

Boulogne is a town cut in two by the River Liane which meanders its way to the coast through a valley in the surrounding hills. What level ground there is near the harbour basins is small in area and hemmed in by higher ground which, especially to the east, rises steeply above the coast road. Even in 1940, buildings such as the customs sheds, numerous other warehouses and the buildings of the fish market congested the harbour area. From the harbour to the east the town climbed the steep hill up to the ancient walled Haute Ville or Citadel. Beyond the Haute Ville the road to Desvres hauled its way up another long rise to the village of St. Martin Boulogne which lay in the shadow of the glowering heights of Mont Lambert. To the west of the Liane, beyond a line between Outreau and the cliffs of Le Portel on the coast, lay more undulating high ground The nature of the high rolling ground incised with steep valleys and undulations, and the fact that he had just two battalions with which to defend the town, concentrated Fox-Pitt's mind. He did not have the manpower to hold a

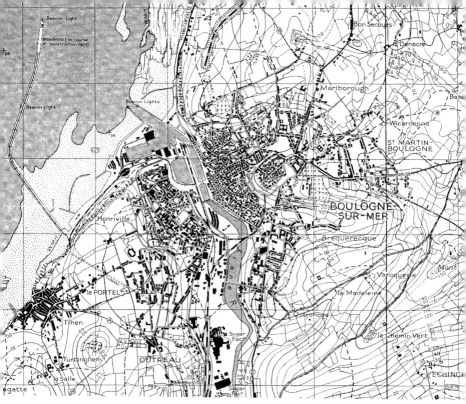

A contemporary map of Boulogne. Courtesy Institut Geographique National

perimeter well outside the town, indeed the undulating nature of the ground offering many hidden approaches along with commanding heights, was ideal tank country. Neither did he wish to reduce his frontage by holding a perimeter within the town and run the risk of his force becoming embroiled in the very worst kind of infantry action – a street fight in a built up area. Fox-Pitt decided that he would hold a line 'guarding the entrances to the town and...along the edge of it...as affording the best anti-tank obstacle.' He determined to fight for the surrounding hills for once they fell Boulogne would be at the mercy of the German panzers. Even so the perimeter chosen was approximately twelve kilometres in length, a staggering distance for just two battalions without transport. The River Liane naturally divided the perimeter in two; all that remained was to decide which battalion would hold which flank. The Welsh Guards had sailed with a strength of 972 of all ranks, although forty-eight were attached to HQ 20 Brigade, the Irish had 720 and since the perimeter to the east of the River Liane was greater than that to the west the allocation of sectors came as no surprise.

'The Brigadier told us that our job was to hold Boulogne from the enemy until the withdrawal was complete. The Irish Guards were to be on the

right...while we, on the left, should hold from Boulogne out to Mount Lambert and back to the sea. We covered what we could but it was not possible to cover all of the left flank towards Wimereux and the sea. There was no accurate information regarding the enemy, no transport and no artillery or tanks. Any transport found in the street was to be taken and used. Luckily I did find a car, but with no ignition key; however an ingenious person got it to work with the aid of a sardine can opener. Maps were issued but when they were unrolled, they turned out to be maps of Kent with Calais in the bottom right hand corner! We did eventually get two proper maps, but somebody immediately spilled ink over one so that I had the only serviceable one. I could only therefore issue very simple orders to the Company Commanders such as: "Follow the tramlines and when you come to a railway bridge, stop." Or "Go up there past the church and stop at the first crossroads and I will meet you later."' Lieutenant Colonel Sir Alexander Stanier Bt., MC. CO 2 Welsh Guards.[6]

At 11.15 am Lieutenant Colonel Stanier met Brigadier Fox-Pitt at the village of St. Leonard four kilometres south of Boulogne on the road to Samer. He was ordered to hold a triangular perimeter east of the Liane with the river at its base, out along the road which ran north-east, uphill along the crest of the northern slopes of the Ravin de Pont Pitendal from Ostrohove to Varoquerie and up as far as the triangle's apex; the main cross roads north-east of Mont Lambert. Turning the line west from the cross roads near Mont Lambert and back along the Desvres road through St. Martin, blocking as many roads as possible back to the sea, would complete the triangle. The total length of the perimeter was about eight kilometres but with 1 Company not yet arrived the distance was just too great for it to be held effectively. In the event a little under six kilometres was held with the left flank, from a little way west of St. Martin to the sea, left open. 2 Company (Major HMC Jones-Mortimer) would take positions from the Liane to the village of Ostrohove with HQ Company, (Captain R B Hodgkinson) equipped as a rifle company, protecting battalion HQ and the village of Ostrohove itself. 3 Company (Major J C Windsor-Lewis) were to continue the line from Ostrohove up to the cross roads near Mont Lambert. 7 platoon were detailed to hold a cross roads near a café at La Madeleine whilst 9 platoon was to cover the important junction where the minor road from Ostrohove to Rottembert crossed the main Desvres-Boulogne road 500 metres or so north-east of the summit of Mont Lambert. 8 platoon, which included Guardsmen Arthur Boswell and Doug Davies, would cover the cross roads from the north and push sections onto Mont Lambert itself. Captain Jack Higgon's 4 Company would hold the rest of the line from the junction with 3 Company as far as the church in the square of St. Martin, blocking roads and watching the country to the north. On their arrival 1 Company (Captain Cyril Heber-Percy) would take up position to

55

the left of 4 Company and block the many roads and tracks around the church in St. Martin.

By the time Lieutenant Colonel Stanier had received his orders from Brigadier Fox-Pitt, 2 and 4 Companies were already on their way from the docks, marching out to their first rendezvous in St. Leonard. For the men of 4 Company the march would take them almost the entire length of the battalion perimeter under trying circumstances until they finally arrived in their allotted sector. Second Lieutenant Peter Hanbury recalled that everyone filled their packs with bully beef and began their march from the harbour through crowds of refugees and a rabble of retreating troops. As the men settled down they began to sing in time honoured Welsh tradition much to the surprise of the fleeing refugees.

'We were all very tired and hungry. The officers had not eaten or slept except for a packet of biscuits and one hour's sleep on the boat. After about an hour's marching we halted opposite some French heavy artillery, which appeared to be abandoned (They were huge, very primitive guns operated by driving in a wedge to raise or lower the barrel – I think from a museum.) we marched up a narrow, congested lane, and eventually reached our positions. I was in reserve and succeeded in borrowing a few shovels from the inhabitants and started digging in. PSM Hooks dug like hell; Sgts. Cook and Holder were very efficient. This was about 4 o'clock.' Second Lieutenant Peter Hanbury. OC 12 Platoon, 4 Company, 2 Welsh Guards. [7]

Guardsman Charles Thompson was one of the men in Peter Hanbury's platoon whilst Syd Pritchard in 11 Platoon, found the march especially taxing.

'On leaving the centre of Boulogne and reaching the top of the long hill where the houses became spread out and with open country ahead I saw the road crowded with every kind of transport, people on foot, bicycles and anything that could carry a few belongings; an occasional soldier, some still carrying a rifle whilst others were unshaven, weary with all the fight knocked out of them but evidently some ack-ack men manning the guns were resisting. They had a German plane in trouble having encircled it with bursting shells. The inevitable happened and the plane was hit. Down it came with smoke trailing behind, one less to harass the retreating column. It was not long before heavy German guns could be heard clearly and shortly afterwards rifle and machine-gun fire. We were allocated a position on the breast of a hill in open country overlooking a wide valley. My trench was in a forward position with a good view over the valley and by late afternoon everyone was ready to meet an attack should one come.'
Guardsman Charles Thompson. 12 Platoon, 4 Company, 2 Welsh Guards. [8]

'We were the last to leave the harbour after all the other companies had been distributed in the town and we were told to get to St. Martin. For some reason or another our machine-gunner had vanished. Our Sergeant got

2 IRISH
GUARDS
Initial positions
pm 22 May

2 WELSH
GUARDS
Initial positions
pm 22 May

landed with the gun and I got landed with the tripod – a heavy old thing. I was carrying that through Boulogne and I remember I tripped over something, put my knee out, and I was limping but I had to forget it – had to march, passing 2 Company on our left. They were digging in in a swede field or a potato field. Anyway we were up on a bank and "Jeff" shouted to me – he'd been transferred to 2 Company – and he said, "bloody see you in Blighty" and we carried on to St. Martin and were detailed off to do this and that. Our corporal had vanished and some time during the afternoon I was told to take over an anti-tank gun. I said "I've never fired the damn thing." I was told "you won't have to worry, there's one in the breech and one other round by your side." If you missed with the first you wouldn't

57

have time for the second one! We had two rounds! We were told to dig in which we did not far from the church, around the corner. I remember a water pump in the village. That evening I went out with Captain Coombe-Tennant and Sergeant Hendry after dark on a reconnaissance and we came up against a lot of French refugees. Coombe-Tennant could speak French and he explained to them who we were. I was instructed to bring them back to HQ and hand them over – our password was "Tower of London" – and then went back to join Coombe-Tennant and the Sergeant.

Guardsman Syd Pritchard. 4 Company, 2 Welsh Guards.[9]

The men of 3 Company found that their march took them furthest from the town and into a sharp arrow-head of a salient with its tip pointing east down the road to Desvres in the shadow of Mont Lambert. The road was one of the main routes into Boulogne from the east and an obvious line of advance for armour. Guardsmen Doug Davies, Arthur Boswell and the best part of 8 Platoon found themselves to be metaphorically, and shortly to be quite literally, at the sharp end of the Welsh Guards line.

'The first night, Wednesday night, I'll always remember it, 3 Company were immediately sent out and we went straight up as far as possible, marched and marched. Our first position was just lying flat on the ground. Then after that you dug in wherever you could – slit trenches – so you'd dive into one of them. I remember two of us lying in a corner looking at what we'd dug – cold night it was – and we just lay there all night looking at nothing but then there again the Germans weren't far away because the next morning they shot us up. The platoon took positions around and that's all I remember about anything organised. I didn't even know who was in charge. I was just told to go 'over there' with another bloke and take up a position.'

Guardsman Doug Davies. 8 Platoon, 3 Company, 2 Welsh Guards.[10]

Arthur Boswell remembers moving out along the Liane's eastern bank, taking a left turn and marching in single file up a narrow road on the outskirts of the town and into 'open country.'

'At times the troops were ordered to "dig in" and then to "move on'. Moving forward to a crossroads, the troops were deployed and dug-in to weapon pits, staggered in design and for one or two soldiers per dug-out. It was then that Sergeant Tom Pennington another guardsman and me were sent forward to higher ground as a forward outpost. After a very near miss of a bomb, we were recalled to join the line of dug-outs. Back in our dug-outs we watched as an unending stream of refugees passed through our lines heading for Boulogne.'

Guardsman Arthur Boswell. 8 Platoon, 3 Company, 2 Welsh Guards.[11]

Corporal Joseph Bryan was helping to man one of a group of three 25mm anti-tank guns under overall command of Lance Sergeant William Green from Bargoed in Glamorgan. Green's gun was one of six from 20 Brigade anti-tank company allotted to 2 Welsh Guards. Due to the difficulties in finding transport at the docks they were late arriving but as soon as they appeared they were deployed in support of the forward companies.

'When we arrived we had with us three old fashioned French guns. They were more like a farmer's plough with iron wheels and a metal seat, they couldn't be towed they had to be man handled. We loaded these onto a flat-topped truck and proceeded inland a little bit then we turned towards the north. We stopped at a place which was elevated from the town, in a kind of a lane, and we set up there looking into a long green valley. There were two or three houses on the left hand side of the lane but the grass and everything was beautiful to look at. Sergeant Green placed his two guns near to two clumps of bushes and I put mine near a wall which I guess was originally a kind of sports field, there was a beautiful lawn inside and a kind of a tower there – I think it might have been used as a broadcast tower at one time or another. It was right out in the country, just as you would picture a road out of any English village.'

Corporal Joseph Bryan. 2 Welsh Guards attached 20 Guards Brigade Anti-Tank Company.[12]

Owing to the length of the perimeter it was impossible to site the guns in any depth and a lack of tools meant that only the gun crews could dig themselves in. The guns had to be hauled behind whatever meagre cover was available, a state of affairs which was to have disastrous consequences for Sergeant Green and the men of the anti-tank crews once spotted by the Germans.

As he toured the line during the afternoon in his requisitioned car, Lieutenant Colonel Stanier became only too aware that his battalion's deployment left a lot to be desired. 1 Company had arrived in position at

'Unending streams of refugees' – the innocent victims of war.

around 3.30 pm and had dug in amongst the gardens and back lanes around the church at St. Martin just north of the junction of the roads to St. Omer and Desvres. Stanier had instructed his company commanders to hold all the main crossroads but there were huge gaps between positions.

'We held the main crossroads. There were foxholes of about three men – rather like the First War – but no communication with them. They didn't link up with fire all around. Others made barricades on the roads; with furniture I'm afraid which was the only thing we'd got. We had too big a front but if we went further back then we lost touch by the houses.'

Lieutenant Colonel Sir Alexander Stanier Bt., MC. CO 2 Welsh Guards.[13]

Bearing in mind all the difficulties and the certainty that there was 'dead ground' between platoons and companies; Stanier felt that his observation was quite good. At least the Germans could not approach down the main road through the village of Mont Lambert or over the tracks and open fields without showing themselves.

Meanwhile, on the other side of the River Liane, the Irish Guards had been marching in single file up through Outreau to a line which described an inverted arc of three and a half kilometres stretching from the village of Manihen on the banks of the Liane to positions overlooking the harbour breakwater just north of Le Portel on the coast. With 1 Company (Captain Conolly R McCausland MC) not yet arrived, 4 Company (Captain L D Murphy) held the high ground on the battalion's left flank around the triangulation point and reservoir south of Outreau, an area known as the Tour de Renard. 2 Company (Captain J W R Madden) was to their right holding the village of Outreau and the line up to the main road to Le Portel and the junction with 3 Company (Captain C K Finlay). The line from the main road to the coast, covering all tracks and approaches from the south was the responsibility of 3 Company.

The Irish Guards Chaplain, Father Julian Stoner, recalled the men reaching the centre of Outreau and falling out to rest on pavements and smoke while Lieutenant Colonel Haydon escorted his company commanders around their positions. There was a bakery in the main square and the delicious smell of freshly baked bread wafted across to the starving Irish. He watched longingly as a French woman handed out long loaves of bread to a crowd of Belgian soldiers but although famished, none of the Irish Guards joined in and a man in Father Stoner's position could hardly be seen to be the first.

It was hunger which almost led to Sergeant Arthur Evans getting lost. Moving off from the docks he and his comrades had driven into town and assembled in Place Dalton next to the church of St. Nicolas just off the Grand Rue to await orders.

'During this interval I walked around to the back of a restaurant [Chez Alfred] to see if a meal could be rustled up for the lads. But despite some

60

arguing – some in English and some in French – they did not want to know. I retraced my steps and to my horror and surprise the square was empty. My platoon had driven off without me. I hitched a ride on a passing Army truck to catch them up but on the outskirts of Wimereux I learned that ...their destination was Calais, where they planned to embark for the UK. Somehow or other I made my way back to the port and by mid-afternoon I was re-united with my platoon. Much to my chagrin, it appeared my absence had not been noticed.'

Arthur Evans found that his platoon had been divided in two. His half, with two guns, was covering the main road through Outreau to the port with the other two guns responsible for covering the coast road at the junction between 2 and 3 Company.

'We had an ideal line of fire and were facing a right hand bend about 400 yards away. Immediately in front of us was a low stone wall about two and a half feet high. Behind us were some houses.'

Sergeant Arthur Evans, 2 i/c Anti-Tank Platoon, 2 Irish Guards.[14]

All along the Irish line the men could hear the gunfire growing louder. Most of them had learned a hard lesson from the Hook of Holland expedition and had 'dug like beavers', quickly and deeply with the picks and shovels each section had been made to carry once their positions had been finalised. Even so the years of restricted peacetime training had left its mark. One Guardsman turned to his platoon commander and asked, 'Are we allowed in these gardens, sir or are they out of bounds?'

Men of the German motorcycle unit of the 2 Panzer Division take a break before continuing their incredible odyssey.

By 1.00 pm the men of 2, 3 and 4 Companies were as ready as they ever would be. 1 Company was on its way after landing and it would be squeezed into the line on the extreme left flank between the Liane and in advance of the forward platoons of 4 Company. By the time Arthur Evans had moved into position the French units at Samer and Neufchâtel were fighting for their lives against the Germans.

Before mid-afternoon Lieutenant Colonel Haydon had begun to receive reports of lone German 'vehicles' sighted on the high ground south of Outreau. To the south somewhere, just over the horizon, the rumbling gunfire told the Irish that the rest of 2 Panzer Division were close behind. Brigadier Fox-Pitt ordered an officers' patrol to move south to establish exactly the positions of the units of the French 21 Division and those of the advancing Germans. Lieutenant Peter Reynolds, son of Major Douglas Reynolds of the Royal Field Artillery who had won the VC near Le Cateau in August 1914 and died two years later, borrowed a car and offered to drive south. Accompanied by three guardsmen in the back and two motor cycle despatch riders (DRs) he set off into the unknown. The patrol reappeared about an hour later unscathed. Reynolds had seen neither hide nor hair of the French or indeed the Germans for that matter but he did report that he had been shot at from a wood just north of Nesles.

Even so the presence of lone German vehicles on the hills to the south was proof that the Germans were within sight of Boulogne. These were just the scouts, others were sure to follow and the men on the left flank of the Irish line would be the first to receive them.

1. Guardsman Syd Pritchard. 11 Platoon, 4 Company, 2 Welsh Guards. Author's tape transcript.
2. Sergeant Arthur Evans, 2 i/c Anti-Tank Platoon, 2 Irish Guards. *Sojourn in Silesia.*
3. Lieutenant Colonel Sir Alexander Stanier Bt, MC. CO 2 Welsh Guards. *Gort's Army – The British Expeditionary Force of 1939-1940.* IWM Sound Archive – 7175/7.
4. Second Lieutenant Peter Hanbury. OC 12 Platoon, 4 Company, 2 Welsh Guards. *A Not Very Military Experience.*
5. *ibid.*
6. Lieutenant Colonel Sir Alexander Stanier Bt., MC. OC 2 Welsh Guards. *Sammy's Wars.*
7. Second Lieutenant Peter Hanbury. *op.cit.*
8. Guardsman Charles Thompson. 12 Platoon, 4 Company, 2 Welsh Guards. Written account sent to author.
9. Guardsman Syd Pritchard. *op.cit.*
10. Guardsman Doug Davies. 8 Platoon, 3 Company, 2 Welsh Guards. Author's tape transcript.
11. Guardsman Arthur Boswell. 8 Platoon, 3 Company, 2 Welsh Guards. Written account sent to author.
12. Corporal Joseph Bryan. 2 Welsh Guards attached 20 Guards Brigade Anti-Tank Company. Author's tape transcript.
13. Lieutenant Colonel Sir Alexander Stanier Bt, MC. *op.cit.*
14. Sergeant Arthur Evans. *op.cit.*

CHAPTER FIVE

THEN THE PANZER SHALL BECOME OUR IRON GRAVE

The German 2 Panzer Division boasted a proud military pedigree. Initially the units of the division had come from garrisons in central Germany but from the autumn of 1938 its recruits were drawn mainly from Bavaria and Austria. As the division's HQ was in Vienna it became known in Army circles as 2 (Wiener) Panzer Division. General Heinz Guderian himself had been its first commanding officer from the division's formation in October 1935 until February 1938 when he moved on to take command of XIX *Korps* and handed the reins of command to *Generalleutnant* Rudolf Veiel. Veiel had served in 2 Panzer Division under Guderian as the commanding officer of 2 Schützen Brigade so he was well aware of his

Generalmajor von Prittwitz takes the salute of the motorcycle battalion of 2 Panzer Division before the war. Courtesy Franz Steinzer

**Generalleutnant Rudolf Veiel
Commander of
2 Panzer Division**

**Oberst von Vaerst
Commander of
2 Schützen Brigade**

Courtesy Franz Steinzer

superior's philosophy of mechanised warfare and deployed his forces in two 'combat groups' for the assault on Boulogne.

From their positions on the line of the Canche, Veiel ordered Combat Group von Prittwitz, (commander of 2 Panzer Brigade), to advance up the coast road via Etaples and attack the southern quarters of Boulogne, west of the River Liane. Combat Group von Vaerst, (commander of 2 Schützen Brigade), was to advance up the N1 from Montreuil to Samer and thence to Baincthun in the hope of encircling Boulogne from the east and north-east.

The columns began their advance at noon and three hours later it was the Irish who first saw isolated scout vehicles of Combat Group von Prittwitz on the high ground south of Outreau opposite the forward platoon of 4 Company under Lieutenant Peter Reynolds holding the area around la Tour de Renard. The German advance had not been without incident however, for both columns had suffered casualties due to a combination of Allied air raids and desperate French resistance. Major M Baron von Sußkind-Schwendi, commanding Tank Destroyer Battalion 38, had one company attached to Combat Group von Prittwitz and the rest advancing towards Samer with Combat Group von Vaerst. On the road between Montreuil and Samer he received news of the destruction of his entire battalion staff.

'*Near Samer, along the street of advance, abandoned French, Belgian and Dutch military vehicles of all kinds were packed together with civilian cars between them. The Staff of the battalion was stopped in Fliegermarchtiefe* [air raid marching order] *in the street. At the head of the advancing division fighting had broken out; the units following had to stop. On a motorcycle with*

A squadron of Blenheim bombers in tight formation. Attempts to slow the German Blitzkrieg by air attacks proved fruitless.

sidecar I had driven to the front to see the situation and to prepare should any parts of the battalion be brought into action. Some kilometres off I saw a close formation of planes flying in the direction of our advance. Because we had hitherto only seen our own planes in close formation I thought them to be friendly too. Shortly after having seen them another commander came from behind and told me, as he overtook me, that the whole Staff of Tank Destroyer Battalion 38 had fallen victim to an enemy air attack. Because the situation ahead had been cleared I immediately returned...A lot of motor vehicles, among them my command car, were still burning. Bombs had hit enemy cars at the roadside and their ammunition and fuel were set on fire

RAF Fairey Battles shooting up a German column during the advance westward in May 1940.

Major Freiherr von Sußkind-Schwendi Commanding Panzer Jäger Battalion 38.
Courtesy Franz Steinzer

and partly exploded. There were bitter casualties; fifteen dead and thirteen wounded of the staff and signals platoon. On my return the wounded were already bandaged and one man was digging the graves for the fallen comrades.'

Major M Th. Freiherr (Baron) von
Sußkind-Schwendi, OC 38 Tank Destroyer
Battalion, 2 Panzer Division.[1]

The RAF was doing its utmost to hinder the German advance on Boulogne. Fighters were patrolling the coastal zone and during the course of the day eleven Westland Lysanders were in action, along with seventy light bombers of which twelve were Fairey Battles and fifty-eight were Bristol Blenheims. Four British aircraft were lost whilst the *Luftwaffe* recorded twenty-four machines destroyed and six damaged during 22 May.

The advance of Combat Group von Vaerst. *Top*: **wrecked Allied vehicles line the road near Samer.** *Right*: **burning vehicles of the staff of Panzer Jäger Battalion 38. The losses amounted to 15 dead, 13 wounded.**
Courtesy Franz Steinzer

The advance of Combat Group von Prittwitz. The crossroads at Neufchâtel. A panzer MkIII receives a direct hit from a French gun.
Courtesy Franz Steinzer

On the coast road too the Germans had run into trouble. *Oberleutnant* Rudolf Behr's platoon of panzers was one of the leading elements of the southern column.

'*The advance continues...A look at the map tells me that we approach a little town Nesles-Neufchâtel. Soon we arrive at the first houses. A long street opens itself when, 300 metres away we see the lightning of a muzzle flash. A split second later we are ready for action. The "car" [panzer] stands, the shot is heard, the shell hits the target, the shield of a French 75mm howitzer, and breaks a piece off. Still movements are seen. A second shell against the gun crew. A third scores a direct hit on the muzzle. The barrel is ripped open. We are approaching the town centre, an open square which five streets run into. Again barricades are to be seen; Frenchmen running up and down. Our leading panzer "Jochen II" fights a duel with an anti-tank gun and I aim at a French 75 mm field gun. In the mean time the leading panzer has advanced to the open square, standing there shooting; my panzer is ten metres behind. Shooting from left, dust from right, ahead I see a muzzle flash. Which target to aim for first? Where are they, the small, well-camouflaged anti-tank guns of the French? There's no time for long consideration. While I feverishly try to discover the positions of the anti-tank gun I see a little cloud of dust and smoke rise up from the panzer ahead. That was a hit! Next moment the hatches are opened, the panzer commander drags himself out and falls down to the rear and remains on the ground at the cross roads. Two other men of the crew dismount and*

67

run behind my "car". In the next second my panzer is trembling from a hard metallic blow, the combat compartment is full of sparks as from a rocket during a firework display. The driver is slumped downward his head hangs forward. In the gloom and still dazed I perceive blood running over his face. There is nothing for it but to get out. The gun aimer though wounded too still has the presence of mind to crank the turret to the side so that the hatch is turned away from the enemy. I call to the driver, he does not move. We dismount raked by hostile MG fire. We take cover behind the panzer. The crossroads becomes an inferno. Again, MG fire. Into a shed. A few hundred metres behind I meet the battalion commander. I report the resistance on the crossing and the loss of my vehicles...I borrow a pistol and stalk ahead. It is impossible to approach the crossroads. It is totally swept by fire but my wounded are still lying there. The rear companies are deployed in outflanking and the tenacious resistance is broken after more than an hour. We are at our disabled cars. My brave driver, the best and most plucky driver of the company is still sitting on his seat as we have left him. In the foremost panzer, an Obergefreiter is lying dead; the wireless operator has lost one foot and is heavily wounded in the leg. The vehicle burns. A corporal manages the near impossible: with a gas mask he enters the crew compartment and pulls out the wounded wireless operator. The "car" is lost. Every attempt to extinguish the fire fails. With enormous crackling of exploding ammunition the panzer burns out, with the dead gun aimer in it, whom we could not save. For him in the real sense of the word his panzer became his iron grave. We bury our dead in a garden a few metres from the place where they had fallen.' Oberleutnant Rudolf Behr.[2]

With two of his three panzers written off, Behr's third 'car' led the advance when it resumed. Eleven kilometres further on lay the suburb of Manihen just south of Outreau. In the centre of Manihen the road forked to left and right. The left fork led uphill towards the centre of Outreau itself whilst the right fork funnelled traffic along the low road close to the banks of the Liane, hemmed in by a steep ridge to the west and the railway line to the east. It was the only road direct to the harbour on the west bank of the Liane with little possibility of manoeuvre for tanks once they were moving along it. Watching, waiting and listening round one of the bends on that low road and intermingled with sections of the forward platoon of 1 Company, lay Sergeant Arthur Evans and the crew of his anti-tank gun. On reaching the fork in the road in Manihen just one kilometre away from Arthur Evans, Rudolf Behr would give the order for his leading panzer to turn right.

No sooner had 1 Company arrived to fill the gap on the left of the Irish Guards line covering both roads leading from the fork in Manihen between the Liane and the right flank of 4 Company at the Tour de Renard, than the Germans arrived. It was half past three and Captain Conolly McCausland's

The crossroads at Neufchatel. The panzer burns. Courtesy Franz Steinzer

men, in advance of the rest of the battalion, had barely begun to break the ground for their trenches when the first shells began to land amongst them. The first desultory bombardment caused more discomfort than real damage – the German guns appeared to be searching for the other anti-tank gun covering the roads to the port, causing it to be moved to a less favourable position – but by 5.30 pm the Germans had hauled field artillery onto the hills to the south and put down a heavy barrage on 1 Company positions. Behind the curtain of shells along the low road from the direction of Manihen came light tanks with infantry in support.

'All day we had heard the rumblings of gunfire but now – about 5.00 pm – it was growing much louder and nearer. Surprisingly, a private car containing some Frenchmen drove at speed past our position and round a bend towards the Germans. Perhaps we should have fired at it but it all happened so quickly. We soon had more serious maters to occupy our minds. The distinct rumbling of tanks could be heard approaching our position and, sure enough, one appeared unconcernedly round the bend and then stopped. I could clearly see the tank commander's head above the open turret with field glasses to his eyes. We opened fire and the tank rocked as we scored two direct hits. The crew baled out and abandoned it. Soon a second appeared and that, too, was effectively disposed of.'

Sergeant Arthur Evans, 2 i/c Anti-Tank Platoon, 2 Irish Guards. Attached 20 Guards Brigade.

'In Manihen...hardly had the panzer turned out of a curve into a straight, when a flash erupts, a blow! Anti-tank gun strike! The panzer commander, a gefreiter, *just having observed the well hidden anti-tank gun is willing to fire and orders the driver to stop. But the "car" rolls further on; rolls further on without the driving human hand because the driver is sitting below, dead from the first shell. His foot is lying on the*

French troops manning a 25mm Hotchkiss anti-tank gun.

pedal. A wall at the side of the road partly falls down because of the impact of the rolling panzer, but then the vehicle stops. Soon other shells hit the iron skin of the panzer, partially going through into the combat compartment. Dismount! Despite some wounds the men succeed in leaving the "car", all except the wireless operator who has a stroke of bad luck. Almost out of danger, he is hit by a MG bullet. Head shot! He too is dead. My platoon is left mourning four dead, three heavily wounded and three lightly wounded this afternoon of 22 May. A painful balance sheet.'
Oberleutnant **Rudolf Behr** [4]

'While congratulating ourselves on our success we came under fire – from motorcycle troops who had been accompanying the tanks. In my mind's eye I can see them now...jumping over low stone walls about two hundred yards away. We exchanged fire with our rifles as well as the guns...A cause for concern was the sight of German infantry manoeuvring around our flanks. From the absence of defensive fire it appeared that we had no supporting troops either side of us. We were stuck out on a limb!'
Sergeant Arthur Evans, 2 i/c Anti-Tank Platoon, 2 Irish Guards. Attached 20 Guards Brigade.[5]

The Germans attacked the advance platoon of 1 Company on the low road at the same time as they moved towards Evans. The fighting in and amongst the back gardens and hedgerows was a chaotic and confused affair, which dragged on intermittently until nightfall as the Germans probed the left flank of the Irish line in an attempt to prise open the lower road into town. A little after 6.00 pm another platoon of 1 Company was attacked under cover of an air raid on Outreau and the Germans succeeded in effectively isolating the advance platoon on the low road from the remainder of the company. At this point the fighting died down for some two hours but the reason for this became apparent at about 8.15 pm when the Germans began a heavy bombardment of the entire battalion front which was to last well into the early hours of 23 May. After dark and towards 10.00 pm the Germans launched their third and final attack of the day on 1 Company positions and completely overran two sections of the forward platoon on the left flank causing heavy casualties. A third section led by Lance Corporal Mawhinney managed to extricate itself from under the nose of a panzer just thirty metres away, Guardsman Montgomery selflessly covering the withdrawal with his Bren gun. Mawhinney later received the Military Medal for his leadership during this action. *Oberleutnant* Künzel, a German motorcycle platoon commander, had been following the panzers towards Boulogne.

'Late in the afternoon we are...in Outreau. The tanks ahead closely followed by the motorcyclists. Suddenly the advance stops. From ahead a vicious sound of fighting can be heard; the sharp bark of our 20mm guns and furious machine-gun fire from the tanks. In between there are dull, heavy thuds. An enemy anti-tank gun? Soon a dispatch rider dashes up. "Motor cyclists forward." In a flash we dismount and are worming our way forward under cover on both sides of the houses. About twelve metres ahead the road bends sharply to the left. There stand two of our own tanks, hit by the enemy anti-tank gun. A tank Leutnant explains the situation: round the bend are two anti-tank guns lying in ambush which cover the whole road and which cannot be put out of action by direct fire. We shall and must capture these guns, so that the advance may go on...The Company Commander puts one platoon in on the left of the road and one on the right, to take the enemy gun from both sides at once...No. 3 platoon vanishes into the houses on the right, and for us the job begins with getting through a thick hedge. In two minutes we have got through, one by one; and we deploy for an attack. We creep unseen almost to the ridge – just in time to see the flash of a shot from the direction of the enemy's position...did that one catch No. 3 platoon which had a shorter journey than we? Section No. 1 gets its machine-gun into position and fires a burst. At that moment the fat is in the fire. The houses ahead of us and the little wood are occupied by the enemy...Burst after burst of machine-gun fire comes whipping into the long green grass. We fall flat in the thorns and nettles while the bullets whistle over us. Where are the bastards? We can't find where the shots are coming from. It seems to be a field fortification, as if there were not enough to deal with already! We have found that a direct attack on the enemy anti-tank guns is impossible. Meanwhile it has grown dark. Every attempt to get within grenade throwing distance fails because of his defensive fire. Corporal B. is killed in trying to locate the enemy machine-gun...The enemy is shooting too damned well. We manage twice more to get in a series of

71

shots at the anti-tank position, when suddenly we hear several sharp explosions and shouting. Then all is quiet at the gun position. I shout across to find out if No. 3 Platoon has reached the objective. Sergeant H. replies that it has been taken. The enemy's left flank was weakly protected, but in our sector he had dug strong defences. The men of No. 3 Platoon had managed to get unseen within grenade throwing distance and to capture the two anti-tank guns. In doing so Leutnant B. was severely wounded.'
Oberleutnant **Künzel**[6]

Arthur Evans also recalled the events of those last few moments as resistance was suddenly brought to a dramatic conclusion.

'There was a deafening explosion, the blast from which knocked me to the ground. My first thought was that one of our guns had blown up. But then I noticed the 'potato mashers' – German hand grenades – sailing through the air towards our position. We were in imminent danger of being surrounded; so I gave the order to disable the guns and withdraw...Dusk was approaching as we crept silently over fields and allotments towards the port, never once meeting any of our own troops. All was quiet. The firing had stopped. Towards midnight we arrived at a large shed and bedded down until daylight. A sentry system was organised. For the past hour or so I had become aware of a pain in my left ankle which was rapidly worsening. I assumed my foot may have been struck by loose pebbles when I was knocked to the ground. On removing my boot my hand came away covered in blood. My sock was soaked. For the moment there was nothing for it but to replace the boot, which was a problem for my ankle had swollen.' **Sergeant Arthur Evans, 2 i/c Anti-Tank Platoon, 2 Irish Guards. Attached 20 Guards Brigade.** [7]

With the capture of the two anti-tank guns and the virtual destruction of the forward platoon of 1 Company the low road into Boulogne had been partially opened. Lieutenant Colonel Haydon had every reason to expect that the Germans would attempt to press their advantage and move men through the breach in the Irish line under cover of darkness rather than wait until dawn and risk coming under fire from the remaining platoons under Captain McCausland's command. There was little doubt that the Irish position was precarious. Haydon's main priority was to restore his left flank but he knew he would not be able to get a true picture of the position until daylight. Even so, he also knew that he would have difficulty in rectifying the situation. His front was so extended that all four rifle companies were in the front line and he had already ordered the carrier platoon, the only mobile element of his force, up into Outreau to block all roads behind 1 Company to counter any German infiltration. Haydon's only 'reserves' were units such as the mortar platoon and signallers whose specialised training made them unsuitable for use in a counter-attack and who were anyhow employed in defending Battalion HQ. In any event there were no field guns, mortars or aircraft to support such a venture so

German infantry during the campaign in the West, May 1940.

the Irish could do little but wait anxiously for the Germans to renew their onslaught. Thankfully, they didn't. *Oberleutnant* Künzel for one was exhausted as were the rest of his men. They spent a 'restless' night in a 'most unfavourable position close to the enemy.' Apart from some desultory shelling the sounds of fighting died away from about 11.00 pm but for the Irish, too, the night was uncomfortable and restless. As one day passed into another, Haydon ordered his men to 'stand to' from 2.30 am to 4.30 am in readiness to meet a dawn attack. Crouched in their trenches, fingers on triggers, the Irish waited. Dawn came and the sky lightened. Still the Irish waited. The Germans would come again, of that there was no doubt. It was just a matter of time.

Like the Irish, the Welsh got their first glimpse of isolated German vehicles of Combat Group von Vaerst during the afternoon, both on the crest of the Mont Lambert ridge and probing 1 Company positions from the north-east. 1 Company had arrived in Boulogne some four hours later than the rest of the battalion and it was Lieutenant Colonel Stanier's intention that they move quickly to extend the left flank of the Welsh line from St. Martin towards the coast. Cyril Sutton had been a Welsh Guardsmen for just four months and almost the first thing he saw as he stepped off the boat was a French soldier, 'lying in the gutter with his intestines in his hands'. That, and the fact that 1 Company had been strafed by Stukas whilst awaiting orders on the quayside, had provided Sutton with his 'baptism of fire in spades!' Cyril Sutton, Guardsman F E Smith and his comrades had then been marched up from the harbour to take positions on the left of 4 Company.

'We moved into a lane at the back of some houses, with gardens leading down to the lane. Here, in the gardens, we had to dig individual dug-outs. Two of us then went back to the cookhouse to fetch a vat of tea. On coming back a German scout car appeared at the top of the lane, about 100 yards away. He didn't stop many seconds and then he was gone.'

Guardsman F E Smith. 1 Company 2 Welsh Guards. [8]

Scanning the eastern horizon and the ridgeline through his field glasses, Lieutenant Coloner Stanier was nudged by an excited Guardsman who exclaimed 'I can see the enemy across the valley, I can see his face now!' Shifting his viewpoint Stanier was amused to find that the 'enemy' was a French civilian squatting under a hedge with his trousers around his ankles answering a call of nature. The next image he saw, however, was not so comical. About one kilometre away he observed a German observing him.

'I saw a chap in a hedge with his field glasses looking at us. We fired at him. He went away and then we saw others during the afternoon, odd ones, but jolly difficult to see, I mean they just came up to this hedge on the ridge. Then in the evening they came and probed a little bit with some light tanks. We fired at them and they went away. We think we hit one but I never saw it.' **Lieutenant Colonel Sir Alexander Stanier Bt., MC. OC 2 Welsh Guards.** [9]

At around 6.00 pm German shells from artillery on the other side of Mont Lambert ridge began to fly over the heads of the guardsmen and register on the light railway line which snaked its way from Ostrohove to St. Martin some 500-750 metres behind the Welsh front, and on Boulogne itself. The first German attacks, which were little more than attempts to test the strength of the Welsh resolve and to establish their positions, began at around 7.00 pm and went on sporadically until dusk. 3 and 4 Companies bore the brunt of this initial confrontation.

Second Lieutenant Peter Hanbury saw a German tank come and 'have a look' at Second Lieutenant Eddie Bedingfield's position 750 metres down the Desvres road from the church in St. Martin and then 'clear off'. The tank approached to within 100 metres of Beddingfield's road block using every scrap of cover and it was all the more disconcerting as it had apparently bypassed Guardsmen Arthur Boswell and Alf Logan of 8 Platoon who thought they were blocking the crossroads on the left of 3 Company's line some 500 metres ahead. It was their turn next.

'As the evening moved towards nightfall, a large tank appeared on the rise of the hill a little way in front with the turret open and the tank commander in clear view. "Look Alf", I said, "It must be one of those big French tanks" – they were seen on the cinema news-reels before the war...but it turned out to be a German tank!! In a matter of seconds all Hell broke loose. The baptism of fire of the Twentieth Guards Brigade had begun in earnest! The tank withdrew as the light failed and after some sporadic gunfire an uneasy calm fell across the line.' **Guardsman Arthur Boswell. 8 Platoon, 3 Company, 2 Welsh Guards.** [10]

Corporal Joseph Bryan also saw his first German tank that afternoon.

'Sergeant Green who had been supplied with field glasses, had really scanned the area very carefully and he reported, "Bryan there's a tank down there coming down the valley". The tank was fired on by all three of our A/T guns and as it came towards us it turned left travelling up the hillside and over the top of the hill out of our range. We didn't see anything else that day.'

Corporal Joseph Bryan. 2 Welsh Guards attached 20 Guards Brigade Anti-Tank Company. [11]

Three tanks in all had probed 3 Company positions and what 2 Welsh Guards War Diary called a 'sharp engagement' took place, the Guardsmen being prodigal with both rifle and Bren gun ammunition. On 4 Company front too, there was further action as the light failed.

The heavier guns opened up, whilst small arms fire, now using tracer bullets, increased but there was no direct push towards us. As the evening grew darker the tracer bullets speeding towards our positions gave the impression of shooting stars, picturesque perhaps but much more deadly.

Guardsman Charles Thompson 12 Platoon, 4 Company, 2 Welsh Guards. [12]

As soon as the Welsh returned fire any tanks which had appeared opposite them had appeared to withdraw and the guardsmen believed they were driving them off, but with the benefit of hindsight Lieutenant Colonel Stanier realised that all the Welsh had succeeded in doing was to give away their positions. 'I learnt that lesson' he was to remark at a later date, 'That's exactly what we did...we told them where we were.'

2 Company on the right flank had not been attacked directly but its proximity to the light railway line made for an uncomfortable afternoon and evening as the German guns registered their targets. From their positions the Guards looked down to where the main road to St. Leonard and Pont de Briques crossed a stream before rising over the shoulder of the Mont

Observing the defensive operations of the British.

Lambert spur. At 6.30 pm Second Lieutenant J D Syrett had gone out beyond Pont de Briques with a party of 262 Field Company Royal Engineers (RE) in an attempt to blow up the bridge over the Liane at Hesdigneul les Boulogne eight kilometres to the south-east. The RE also helped 2 Company by cratering the road over the stream flowing down the Ravin de Pont Pittendal just in front of their line and ignited a gas main in the process, the flames from which flickered on their roadblocks throughout the night and created a wonderful marker for the German artillery.

At around 9.00 pm Colonel Deane VC, by then withdrawing from positions around Wimeruex due to reports of German patrols in the area, arrived at battalion HQ and offered the services of his men of the AMPC. In spite of the gesture his offer was not accepted with enthusiasm. The view of the Welsh 'regulars' was that the AMPC were on the whole, 'old, disorganised, tired but keen,' armed only with rifles and little ammunition and with no food of their own, '...their status in the front line was impossible.' Some of the more able were used by Lieutenant Colonel Stanier later to defend Battalion HQ and others took up positions on the left of the Welsh line but the rest were seen as a liability during the dramatic events which were to unfold during the course of the next day at the harbour. Stanier did use 150 men – the exhausted remnants of 8 Durham Light Infantry retiring towards the coast after their battle with 7 Panzer Division at Arras on 21 May – as reserves behind Battalion HQ and 1 Company.

A panzer MkIV of 2 Panzer Division camouflaged against air attack.

As darkness deepened and the firing died down along his front Stanier decided, as a precaution, to move his HQ from the school house in Ostrohove to a cottage at the waterworks 400 metres or so to the rear. It was a move which did not endear him to the local populace. As he returned to the cottage at around 10.00 pm for some much needed supper he was met by his second in command Major John Vigor and the Adjutant Captain Robin Rose-Price both of whom appeared worried.

'The French managing director of the waterworks was apparently extremely angry and wished to see me. He was in a towering rage because, he said, my men had trampled all over his flower beds and rose garden. While he was declaiming loudly and at great speed about our sins, there was a big explosion; I thought we were being shelled but it was only a petrol cooker blowing up with my precious supper on it. Bray the Quartermaster, with great presence of mind, threw an old feather mattress on the flames, which gave off such fumes we had to put our gas masks on. The Frenchman did not have one so he fled, coughing and crying and was not seen again.'

Lieutenant Colonel Sir Alexander Stanier Bt., MC. CO 2 Welsh Guards.[13]

After this unwelcome diversion Lieutenant Colonel Stanier set out once more in his car at 11.00 pm and for the next two hours visited all his companies in the front line. It was a difficult journey, the roads being choked with columns of refugees who also caused much disruption at the Welsh road blocks. Sporadic machine-gun fire could be heard but nothing more and officer patrols were sent out by company commanders in order to establish just where the Germans had gone. Occasionally both sides sent up flares over the valley to the east of St. Martin in the hope of detecting movement. Second Lieutenant Peter Hanbury led one patrol out at around 10.30 pm, accompanied by '...nine good men, Eastment and Sergeant Walker in the rear.'

'I had a feeling of real excitement as I thought we were to surprise a German patrol in the valley. Some rats on a rubbish dump gave us a jump, otherwise it was uneventful. On getting back I went to Co. HQ to report and had something to eat. I got back in time to do rounds at 1.30, and slept from 2.15 until stand-to at 3.30.'

Second Lieutenant Peter Hanbury OC 12 Platoon, 4 Company, 2 Welsh Guards.[14]

After some hours of cat napping in his cramped dug-out Guardsman Arthur Boswell was sent out before dawn with a Corporal and another guardsman to see if the Germans had occupied the nearby village of Mont Lambert one kilometre along the Desvres road. On the way back, Boswell's patrol were creeping soundlessly along a grassy track which skirted a high stone wall when they heard the unmistakable sounds of movement.

'Someone, or something, could be heard plainly, on the other side of the wall and moving in the same direction. A little way ahead a gap in the wall could be seen. The Corporal indicated "safety catches off" and for us to take

77

up a firing position to take on whatever came through the gap. Three French soldiers, weaponless and dishevelled emerged and were very startled to be looking down the business ends of three rifles! The Corporal waved them on.' **Guardsman Arthur Boswell. 8 Platoon, 3 Company, 2 Welsh Guards.**[15]

On returning to 3 Company lines the Corporal reported to Lieutenant Pilcher and Boswell resumed his stint in his trench.

Apart from the Frenchmen not another living soul had been seen by any of the Welsh patrols. The Germans it seemed had disappeared. They were not in Mont Lambert village nor had they been encountered creeping around the valley of St. Martin but nevertheless the men of Combat Group von Vaerst were out there and they were on the move. Already *Oberleutnant* Durkes had driven his 3 Company of 2 Motorcycle Battalion through the Forêt de Boulogne and into the village of la Cappelle on the St. Omer road. The speed of the German advance had so taken the Allies by surprise that just before dusk an extraordinary incident occurred. A car came motoring towards the Germans standing around in the centre of the village and when they halted it a British Major stepped out lightly and greeted them 'cordially'.

'At first we are startled but after a few words the reason for his cordiality becomes evident; he thinks us to be Dutchmen who have managed to struggle their way through to Boulogne! Not until we show our national

The armoured onslaught drives towards Boulogne. Courtesy Franz Steinzer

markings with the swastika does he realise his error – and this vehemently ripens his disillusionment!'

Oberleutnant Durkes OC 3 Company, 2 Motorcycle Rifle Battalion, 2 Panzer Division.[16]

Following in the wake of these forward German units were others, such as Panzer Pioneer Battalion 38, which were moving up to villages like Bainchthun to dismantle Allied road blocks and put up their own to cut off any means of escape.

The German probing during the afternoon and evening of 22 May had succeeded in making the Welsh show their hand. There was little need to attack the Guardsmen during the hours of darkness. They could wait until daylight. Until then von Vaerst could move more men across the face of the Welsh perimeter and swing them west towards the coast.

During the night the Germans moved around the northern suburbs of Boulogne in the direction of Wimereux but encountered stiff French resistance at Fort de la Creche, high on its lofty perch overlooking the harbour and most of the lower town of Boulogne from the north. The old fort, which dated from the nineteenth century, was a desirable prize for the Germans as it offered uninterrupted observation of the lower town right across to Outreau on the other side of the harbour. More importantly, it dominated the harbour and its seaward approaches. Just before midnight on 22 May *Oberleutnant* Durkes advanced from la Capelle to the northern suburbs of Boulogne where he received further orders.

'On the map...about 3 or 4 kilometres away from us in the direction of the sea, an old fortress is drawn. Its present condition, armament and defence are unknown. We the leading company, with the escorting panzers, have to capture the fort by "coup de main". A short briefing with the leader of the panzers and then we start. It is pitch dark. Now – behind a little rise – a dull glittering stripe: The Channel! It is calm and quiet; no breath of air is stirring. We stop and switch off our engines.' *Oberleutnant* Durkes OC 3 Company, 2 Motorcycle Rifle Battalion, 2 Panzer Division.[17]

Unsure of the exact position of the fort Durkes decided to take *Oberfeldwebel* Forster and a handful of men forward on foot but first he arranged a series of signals with the rest of the company: on seeing three green flashes the rest of the company were to advance silently without the panzers and with hand grenades, if three red flashes were seen, however, the panzers were to race to Durkes assistance.

Carefully moving ahead Durkes came up against a barbed wire entanglement which turned out to be an abandoned anti-aircraft gun position. He pressed on and after a few hundred metres reached the railway cutting which, today, still splits the village of Terlincthun in two.

'Close by to the right are the first houses of Terlincthun, so, half right ahead of us must be the fort. Still there is nothing to be seen; it is deadly silent. Now we must find the exact position of the fort; the only aid is the

marching compass. Nestling closely to the railway embankment, hidden under thick shrubs, in scanty light, we fix the marching distance...only 300-400 metres. We advance, ever more cautious, ever more noiseless. Suddenly confused voices: we all take cover. We are lying on a meadow. Only a few paces off a group of soldiers is crossing our path, probably sentry relief from the fort.'

Whilst the Germans lay motionless a motorcycle started up, came towards them then turned off to their right. Further off a hubbub of voices and the clash of weapons could be heard. In the inky blackness more troops passed by just metres away. As Durkes pondered what to do next the angry growling of engines to his rear made his mind up for him.

'The panzers left behind start their engines and drive in our direction; the rest of the company follows with the vehicles. The noise of the engines becomes louder and louder. Gradually to our right the enemy awakes. Well there is the fort! Now – whilst the vehicles are still some way off – a MG starts hammering. Two, three, five soon follow. The fat is in the fire. The panzers answer but it is too dark to deliver well-aimed shots. Moreover a wired earth bank, about four metres high, protects the fort...The enemy fire is growing heavier. Our situation is delicate. Surprise, our main weapon, is lost...we must retreat. Slowly we manage to turn back the motorcycles on

An armoured bridgelayer comes into action on the road to Boulogne. Courtesy Franz Steinzer

French civilians flee Boulogne along the Rue Porte Neuve in the face of the German advance.

the narrow road beside the earth bank. Forster orders the last few vehicles to be pushed back for some hundred metres with engines stopped. So, under covering fire from the panzers we disengage with difficulty. Losses are low, God be praised, but Unteroffizier *Wolf is mortally wounded by a bullet whilst turning his motorcycle.'*

Retiring towards the northern suburbs of Boulogne, Durkes reported the failure to take Fort de la Creche to Colonel von Vaerst personally. Von Vaerst informed Durkes that his company would be needed again to attack the fort early the next morning but this time with artillery support. Until then he was told to rest his men. Exhausted after a long day's journey with some hard riding and hard fighting along the way, Durkes and his company lay down in a broad, straight avenue and within minutes were fast asleep.

The encirclement of the Boulogne garrison was now almost complete. General Heinz Guderian even made his way to the front to see the situation for himself and shortly before 2.00 am on 23 May he returned to the Pont de Briques from the HQ of a forward rifle battalion and sent out a message to 2 Panzer Division; 'Panzer and riflemen secure south of Outreau.' Before Outreau, against the Irish, the Germans had lost many comrades striking

81

at the southern front. For some, their panzers had quite literally, to paraphrase the lyrics of a popular Panzer *Lied* of the time, become their iron grave. If Combat Group von Prittwitz could fight on and seal off Outreau the next day and if the tanks and mechanised infantry in the vanguard of Combat Group von Vaerst could overcome French resistance at Fort de la Creche and reach the coast north of Boulogne, then an iron ring would close around the town, the likely consequence of which would be the destruction of the Allied garrison.

1. Major M T Baron von Sußkind-Schwendi, OC 38 Tank Destroyer Battalion, 2 Panzer Division in Strauss D F J. *Friedens und Kriegserlebnisse einer Generation. Ein Kapitel Weltgeschichte aus der Sicht der Panzerjäger-Abteilung 38(SF) in der ehemaligen 2 (Wiener) Panzerdivision.*

2. *Oberleutnant* Rudolf Behr. *Dann ist uns Panzer ein eisernes Grab* in Guderian Generaloberst H (Ed) *Mit den Panzern in Ost und West.* Vol. 1.

3. Sergeant Arthur Evans. 2 i/c Anti-Tank Platoon, 2 Irish Guards, attached 20 Guards Brigade. *Sojourn in Silesia.*

4. *Oberleutnant* Rudolf Behr. *op.cit.*

5. Sergeant Arthur Evans. *op.cit.*

6.*Oberleutnant* Künzel. Einnahme von Boulogne-sur-Mer in *Militär-Wochenblatt*, No.35, Cols. 1517-1521. (Berlin, 1940).

7. Sergeant Arthur Evans. *op.cit.*

8. Guardsman F E Smith. 1 Company, 2 Welsh Guards. Letter to author.

9. Lieutenant Colonel Sir Alexander Stanier Bt, MC. CO 2 Welsh Guards. *Gort's Army – The British Expeditionary Force of 1939-1940.* IWM Sound Archive – 7175/7.

10. Guardsman Arthur Boswell. 8 Platoon, 3 Company, 2 Welsh Guards. Account sent to author.

11. Corporal Joseph Bryan. 2 Welsh Guards attached 20 Guards Brigade Anti-Tank Company. Author's tape transcript.

12. Guardsman Charles Thompson.12 Platoon, 4 Company, 2 Welsh Guards. Account sent to author.

13. Lieutenant Colonel Sir Alexander Stanier Bt, MC. CO 2 Welsh Guards. *Sammy's Wars.*

14. Second Lieutenant Peter Hanbury OC 12 Platoon, 4 Company, 2 Welsh Guards. *A Not Very Military Experience.*

15. Guardsman Arthur Boswell. *op.cit.*

16. *Oberleutnant* Durkes OC 3 Company, 2 Motorcycle Rifle Battalion, 2 *Panzer* Division in Strauss D F J. *Friedens und Kriegserlebnisse einer Generation. Ein Kapitel Weltgeschichte aus der Sicht der Panzerjäger-Abteilung 38(SF) in der ehemaligen 2 (Wiener) Panzerdivision.*

17. *Oberleutnant* Durkes *ibid.*

CHAPTER SIX

A CHANGE FROM PUBLIC DUTIES

As dawn approached on 23 May the guardsmen of 20 Brigade, who had spent a nervous and uncomfortable night in their trenches posted in open country, could at least give thanks that they had not come under direct attack during the hours of darkness. A little after 1.30 am Brigadier Fox-Pitt had been visited at Brigade HQ by Major General H C Lloyd from Rear GHQ who reassured him once again that a battalion of tanks and 1st Battalion Queen Victoria's Rifles would soon be on their way to reinforce the Boulogne garrison. Fox-Pitt was to be disappointed on that score.

3 Royal Tank Regiment and 1 QVR had indeed landed at Calais but they would soon have more than enough to keep them occupied in defending that port let alone another. Lloyd's assurance was to prove to be a chimera. A few hours later Fox-Pitt had learned that Major General Lloyd had taken ship to England along with General Brownrigg which meant that he was now in undisputed command of operations in Boulogne. This had enabled him to use Colonel Deane's AMPC, which had already been withdrawn from its posts around Rear GHQ in Wimereux amid reports of German units in the area. Some of Deane's men were strung out in posts along the northern suburbs of Boulogne from the left flank of the Welsh line at St. Martin to the coast near the Casino on la Digue Ste. Beuve with the help of

The Casino from the cliffs above the Boulevard Ste. Beuve. Nausicaa, the French National Centre for the Sea, now stands on this site.

remnants of 5 Buffs and the Royal West Kent Regiment, in preparation for a German attack at dawn. The Germans did not attack *en masse* at dawn, however. The German motorcycle infantrymen under *Oberleutnant* Durkes slept on after a hard night's fighting but there were those in the ranks of the Welsh Guards less than two kilometres away to the south-east, who were desperately trying to keep their eyes open.

Guardsman Charles Thompson was already well into his second stint of sentry duty when the first streaks of daylight began to bleach the sky on the morning of 23 May. Within a few metres of his trench was a tall hedge but through gaps in the bushes he could just see into the field beyond and across the valley towards where he thought the Germans lay. Tired as he was, Thompson kept reminding himself that his comrades behind him were relying on him at such a crucial time and would depend on him to rouse them in an emergency. The problem was that a thick mist hugged the ground to his front and he knew it would be impossible to see any movement. In the stillness of the hour before dawn the slightest noise was accentuated and suddenly Thompson felt sure he could hear the sound of

A make-shift bipod for the M34 Spandau machine-gun.

men dragging themselves through the damp grass on the other side of the hedge.

'Try as I may I could not see any movement and I was loathe to open fire until there was a target, on the other hand the resting men had to be warned if the Germans were creeping up on us. Whilst I can say I was not frightened most certainly the hair stood up on the back of my neck, I was very tense and made sure there was a bullet in my rifle breech and my bayonet was fixed. The movement in the field was very slow which perplexed me and I stood a while not understanding the movement when suddenly it dawned on me, being a country man and having a good knowledge of animals, that it was a cow grazing. It was totally unexpected in view of what was happening but the relief was tremendous. On being relieved it was not a matter of having breakfast as 'stand to' was called; the dawn was really breaking.'

Guardsman Charles Thompson.12 Platoon, 4 Company, 2 Welsh Guards.[1]

Brigadier Fox-Pitt had in fact ordered the battalions to 'stand-to' from 3.30 am until 4.30 am. On 4 Company front of the Welsh line Second Lieutenant Hanbury set some of his men to work digging again just before dawn and sent others away to organise a brew of tea. Syd Pritchard in 11 Platoon was also out looking for breakfast.

'I took a tin of Machonachie from my greatcoat pocket, which was under a hedge, and I asked a French lady would she warm it up for me. She slammed the door in my face. A good start! I stripped off and went down to wash and clean my teeth down at the pump and whilst I was there I remember a spotter plane came over. I noticed this fellow and he sort of drew a circle above us and no sooner afterwards "here it comes". They must have already marked us out using this fellow in the spotter plane. Well then "Jerry" started. He decided to let us have it.'

Guardsman Syd Pritchard. 11 Platoon, 4 Company, 2 Welsh Guards.[2]

The time was 7.30 am and the German assault fell simultaneously on both the Welsh and Irish sectors. On the Welsh front Major Windsor Lewis's over extended platoons of 3 Company were the first to suffer. Lieutenant Ralph Pilcher's 8 Platoon in particular, with its nose poking out towards Mont Lambert at the apex of the Welsh line, was the first to feel the force of the German blow, which started with a fusillade of machine gun fire.

'Sergeant Roberts called out, "any volunteers to go for breakfast?" Jack leapt out of his one man dug-out, Alf and I began to climb out of ours when a German machine-gun opened fire. Alf and I slid back into the hole and Jack dropped flat just behind. Alf and I returned fire in the direction of the machine-gunner who could be seen behind a hedge. When the firing abated Jack called out; "Sarge I've been hit.". Alf and I reached over and unceremoniously dragged him into our trench. The anti-tank rifle had been silenced, and then the Bren was only firing single rounds. Thinking they

85

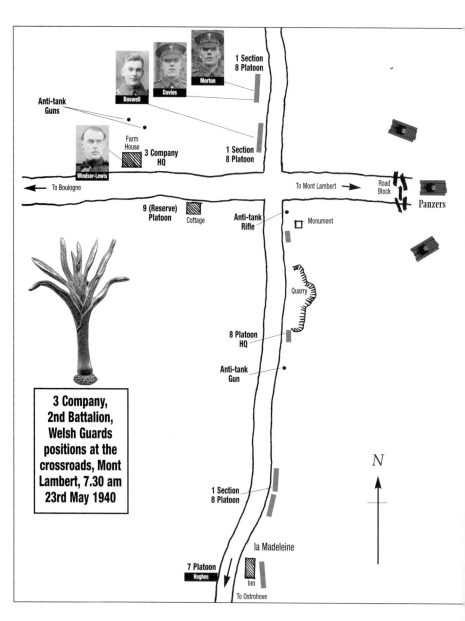

1 Section
8 Platoon

Morton

Davies

Boswell

Anti-tank
Guns

Windsor-Lewis

Farm
House

3 Company
HQ

1 Section
8 Platoon

← To Boulogne

To Mont Lambert →

Road
Block

Panzers

9 (Reserve)
Platoon

Cottage

Anti-tank
Rifle

Monument

Quarry

8 Platoon
HQ

Anti-tank
Gun

N

3 Company,
2nd Battalion,
Welsh Guards
positions at the
crossroads, Mont
Lambert, 7.30 am
23rd May 1940

1 Section
8 Platoon

la Madeleine

7 Platoon
Hughes

Inn

To Ostrohove

were short of 'ammo' I shouted across to Sergeant Tom Pennington, "we've
got some spare mags Sarge... if you want them." "It's alright 'Bos' the gun's
knackered", responded the Sergeant. I then turned to Jack's wounded arm,
and being unable to stand up and offer a tempting target...I sliced open
Jack's battle dress sleeve, pullover and shirt with my army knife. The wound

was through the fleshy part of the forearm and did not appear to have struck the bone. I applied my field dressing to staunch the blood flow and replaced his sleeves.' Guardsman Arthur Boswell. 8 Platoon, 3 Company, 2 Welsh Guards.[3]

Boswell then poked his head up above his parapet to have a quick look around only to be reprimanded by the sonorous and lilting Welsh tones of Guardsman Reece carrying over from another trench, 'Hey Boss-well, keep your flippin' head down boyo, or you'll get the flippin' thing blown off for you.'

Lieutenant Colonel Stanier, out on yet another tour of his positions, had stopped at 3 Company HQ in a farm just west of the Mont Lambert crossroads and was telling Sergeant Williams his driver that the almost endless stream of refugees should be made to stop at the road blocks, when German tanks suddenly advanced from the direction of the village of Mont Lambert.

'As I was there I saw the German tanks come bursting out of the village and start firing at the little anti-tank guns which were just in the hollow below me. They put one or two rather close to the farm where I was. I was peering over the wall. They fired at the men holding the crossroads at Mont Lambert. They burst out of the village one behind the other and spread out. They were in three's; one would be in front and the other two would be looking out either side to protect it. They moved quite fast... they were light tanks.' Lieutenant Colonel Sir Alexander Stanier Bt., MC. CO 2 Welsh Guards. [4]

One of the tanks roared towards the crossroads and poured a hail of machine-gun fire into the abandoned cars, furniture and assorted bric-a-brac which passed for one of the roadblocks, setting it alight. The tank stopped so close to Second Lieutenant Neil Perrins commanding 9 Platoon in reserve near Company HQ, who was out on patrol at the time, that he was able to stand next to it undetected! Even so his patrol suffered casualties as a result of machine-gun fire.

The anti-tank guns manned by Sergeant Green and Corporal Joseph Bryan sited around 3 Company HQ made a spirited response to the tank threat.

'Sergeant Green alerted us all to a tank that was coming down the same track as the other one, but it came a little closer to us. This was stopped – fired on by all three guns and it was stuck there. You could see using the telescopic sights of these old guns – you could see very clearly that one of the occupants had got out and was on the opposite side of the tank crawling on his hands and knees to keep out of the fire. I could hear the PSM instructing people to fire. There was a spotter plane overhead and the amount of fire that went up there – tracers – boy! We loaded it with shots and the plane came down and there was a big cheer. That gave me an indication as to where the rest of the battalion were.' Corporal Joseph Bryan. 2 Welsh Guards attached 20 Guards Brigade Anti-Tank Company.[5]

The fight for the Mont Lambert crossroads. Men of 8 Platoon, 3 Company, 2 Welsh Guards take on the panzers. On the right Captain Hamil Carter is depicted firing his revolver.

After about three quarters of an hour the rest of the German tanks, to those observers on 3 Company front at least, appeared to withdraw. What seemed like a withdrawal from one position however, looked like an outflanking manoeuvre from another. Lieutenant Colonel Stanier saw the tanks 'swerve away to the right as if they were going towards Calais', and then take cover behind hedges only to reappear further down the left flank to threaten first 4 and then 1 Company positions. During a momentary lull in the fighting Stanier left Major Windsor-Lewis and motored to St. Martin to see Captain Cyril Heber-Percy.

'I went with the company commander down a little passageway; Brigadier Fox-Pitt was there as well, and we looked out and saw some tanks. We thought they were British tanks! We couldn't believe that the Germans had been so quick. They'd come round from Number 3 Company and were already down as fast as me motoring down the road. They were belting out as fast as they could and it was all smooth fields. There was nothing to stop them...They were very bold. They were fairly charging about.' Lieutenant Colonel Sir Alexander Stanier Bt., MC. CO 2 Welsh Guards.[6]

88

As the morning wore on the Germans by-passed Pilcher's platoon and began to threaten 3 Company HQ and 9 platoon posts, under Second Lieutenant Perrins, around the farmhouse. Casualties began to mount as the battle grew in ferocity all around. Shelling began in earnest at around 9.00 am, again registering on the light railway running just behind the Welsh line. A house near the Mont Lambert crossroads was blasted by shellfire and reduced to a heap of rubble, igniting a dump of ammunition stored nearby and producing a lethal firework display. The Germans then switched the point of attack to focus on 2 Company and Second Lieutenant Hesketh (Hexie) Hughes's 7 platoon on the extreme right of 3 Company near a café at a road junction in the hamlet of la Madeleine. Whilst German artillery and mortar fire made the Welsh keep their heads down, tanks and mechanised infantry came over the ridge. At around 10.30 am four tanks came over the ridge and headed straight for Second Lieutenant Hexie Hughes's exposed position. In 1940 la Madeleine consisted of little more than four small houses, two cottages and an *estaminet* clustered around a road junction. Unlike most of the other anti-tank guns on the Welsh front Hughes had managed to dig one in to cover the junction with some success. He had another a little way behind. As Hughes watched, one tank advanced towards the junction and began to move behind the *estaminet*.

Another knocked out his second anti-tank gun and soon he noticed two more working their way around him. He reasoned that he would soon be surrounded so he decided to withdraw his platoon back to the other side of the road to secure a better fire position – with fatal results.

'Directly he got up and ran back to take up his position behind he got half his platoon back and half got shot up including him. He was killed. That was moving your position under fire.' Lieutenant Colonel Sir Alexander Stanier Bt., MC. CO 2 Welsh Guards. [7]

The incident proved beyond doubt that the German tanks worked in concert, one or more forcing the Welsh to break cover only to be picked off by another. Stanier later conceded that the German troops were 'very, very well trained.' Those of 7 platoon who had escaped fell back towards Headquarters Company positions in Ostrohove.

By 11.00 am the Welsh on 2 and 3 Companies' front had been in action for some three and a half hours but, with further German attacks falling on Lieutenant R C Sharples's platoon of Headquarters Company, Lieutenant Colonel Stanier decided a readjustment was necessary. One platoon of 2 Company and Company HQ were withdrawn to the left and rear about 300 metres to the line of the light railway. As the remnants of Hexie Hughes's platoon had already retired a message was hurriedly dispatched to 3 Company HQ and remarkably it got through.

'The shelling and firing from the tanks on our front was growing in its intensity. Word reached me by messenger that my right flank was exposed

Captured Guardsmen of 3 Company are put to work digging temporary graves near la Madeleine shortly after the battle near Mont Lambert. Courtesy Herr Franz Steiner

as No. 2 Coy had been forced to withdraw and with my own right forward platoon also compelled to withdraw I decided to retire with what was left of the Coy.' **Major JC Windsor-Lewis OC 3 Company, 2 Welsh Guards.**[8]

Windsor-Lewis retired from his HQ and fell back down the road through St. Martin and then downhill towards the town itself. He finally arrived at the Citadel in the Haute Ville defended by the French garrison under General Lanquetot and sent a message to Brigade HQ telling them where he was.

The withdrawal of 3 Company HQ meant that Second Lieutenant Pilcher's 8 Platoon was albeit surrounded, the Germans having moved around and behind it to follow up Windsor-Lewis's withdrawal and threaten 4 Company's positions in and around St. Martin itself. 8 Platoon was in grave danger of being cut off and, to make matters worse, Guardsman Arthur Boswell could see at least one German tank looking down on them menacingly some 200 metres away on the slopes of Mont Lambert. Orders from Second Lieutenant Pilcher for the men to extricate themselves, one dug-out at a time, were passed along the line.

'Two got through, under the line of tracer bullets, unscathed, but Sergeant Sankey was blasted by a shell which took him – and a barbed wire fence – into the next field. He is believed to have survived albeit minus an arm. Corporal "Wimpey" Williams sprang out of the same dug-out as the Sergeant and dashed through the gap in the fence and dropped alongside the wounded Sergeant to help him... Lieutnant Pilcher then ordered the rest to "stay put". Later the Lieutnant came back and gave the order for the rest of the platoon to come out, "in their own time". I said, "I'll go first then Jack and Alf can follow." I climbed out slowly and after glancing at the menacing tank to see if there was any movement, crawled very slowly towards the comparative safety of the nearby wood. I have never been so scared as I was then- I could feel the hair on the back of my neck curling! Further into the wood I joined Lieutnant Pilcher, Sergeant Pennington, Corporal Webb and others; about twelve in total.*

Guardsman Arthur Boswell. 8 Platoon, 3 Company, 2 Welsh Guards.[9]

*During the next few days, Boswell and his small band led by Lieutenant Pilcher, cut off from their battalion and now behind German lines, decided to make a break towards Wimille and the coast following the 'deeply embedded tracks created by the panzer tanks', in the hope of getting across the Channel. After many amazing adventures and hair raising encounters with German patrols during which, one by one, Lieutenant Pilcher and nine more men were captured, Arthur Boswell and Alf Logan, his one remaining companion, decided to head for Spain and thence Gibralatar. The thought of such a journey was almost laughable but they set out and, as they did so, Arthur Boswell offered up a silent prayer of thanksgiving for sparing him in the recent fighting and for guidance through what lay ahead: 'if He be for us...then who can stand against us?' Boswell's prayers were eventually answered. After an incredible journey the duo reached Britain towards the end of 1941 almost eighteen months after the Boulogne fighting.

Arthur Boswell. Taken whilst on the run in Marseilles.

Courtesy Mr Arthur Boswell

91

'We hadn't a dog's chance. Just the tanks came on with a few infantry behind. They didn't have hordes of people. They didn't need them. When they got to us in Boulogne we were near enough surrounded we could see the tanks on the hills and the infantry sitting around. I remember I was in a slit trench there by myself. A little dog got on my back and they shot that off in no uncertain terms. It was all right for me but they shot the poor little dog off. I just dropped in there and kept my head down until I heard the tanks roll past and then I was up and away. They had tracer bullets and they seemed to come so slowly and then zip past we were fortunate to be able to dive under them. They had everything. We had .303 ammunition, fifty rounds! This friend of mine Doug Morton was killed. He just got shot. You got the feeling that it had to happen to him. He went to Holland and when he came back I went to talk to him and he must have been frightened out of his life. When I heard he'd been killed in Boulogne I wasn't surprised. I don't know why. I was not sure whether Captain Carter was killed, but from then on they came at us. Some silly bugger said we pushed them back – we didn't! Give credit where it's due, the officers and NCO's didn't know what to do. They hadn't a clue. Poor old Major Lewis. After they shot us up, we'd split up completely and then we took a position, two of us, with a Boys anti-tank rifle, on a corner. There were the two of us, a young officer and two other guardsmen and a big lorry. They said "move that lorry across the road". I said "I can't drive that" so they said "oh well you take this Boys anti-tank rifle and get in that slit trench – five rounds only," and they moved the big lorry. What's a lorry? A German officer or whatever he was laughed his head off when we fired at his tank and it bounced off! We'd been told that this Boys anti-tank rifle with .5 bullets was invincible and they weren't. After we'd fired this anti-tank gun and this "Jerry" officer started shooting at us from the tank, I ran that fast I went past the flipping bullets because you could see the tracers! And yet it's strange; in that situation you weren't frightened. From then on we just kept dodging and dodging and diving into shell holes or whatever. The Germans came down and away we went again – only singly. We dribbled our way back. I eventually found my way back dodging the Germans to the fish market.'

Guardsman Doug Davies. 8 Platoon, 3 Company, 2 Welsh Guards.[10]

Captain Hamil Carter, Second in Command of 3 Company, had been seriously wounded in the arm on the road to St. Martin but would survive.

After successfully destroying one tank earlier, Sergeant Green's anti-tank guns had by now been marked as targets as the Germans rolled forward.

'We never heard anything from the battalion. There was no communication whatever between the battalion and us. We were a Sergeant, two Corporals and eight guardsmen. Sergeant Green said "Bryan they are assembling a gun by the side of a haystack." With his field glasses

2 Panzer Division on the move.

he could see them assembling the field gun there. The problem I have with this, is the fact that I believe that was the time to go and leave our guns there to be blown up without our people, but Sergeant Green didn't say anything about that, he just stayed there doing his job. About two hours after he told me they were assembling a gun there was a "boom, boom, boom, boom, boom" and I looked over – we were about twenty yards away from his guns – and the Sergeant and the crews were all in pieces. What bothers me when I think about it is, the battalion was going to withdraw that day, so why weren't we told about the possible withdrawal so that we could have got out of there. There was a Corporal Fowler, he was not in the front line with us but he was stationed in a concrete pill-box type of thing. I assumed he was the contact man either for incoming or outgoing messages but we never received any message. After this explosion, the two guardsmen on my gun ran down the lane and there was all kinds of heavy German MG fire and I thought, well I'll go to where this Corporal. Fowler had been stationed. I ran to his place and I saw that he had left and I could tell which way he'd gone because he'd ran into a meadow and left quite a trail in the meadow so I thought, "that's the way for me." However, after about twenty yards into the meadow there was a different kind of gunfire – more like a .303 being fired – and it was hitting a wall and chipping concrete off. I thought it was just random MG fire so I moved further ahead, still trying to follow the Corporal's track and I lifted my head up to try and get a better idea of where he went and again there was a .303 firing. I decided it was too dangerous to try and go further and I returned to the little blockhouse where Fowler had

93

been. When I got there I did feel a little pain in my leg and I thought I'd been shot but it was a shard of concrete that had been removed from the wall and had gone through my left trouser leg and punctured my calf. I thought I'd better stay away from that area for a while so I wrapped my leg with a field bandage we carried with us and it seemed to heal pretty quickly. I thought I'd try later on to go down the lane where my two guardsmen had gone, however I sat there for about two hours and I must have dozed off and it wasn't until the next morning – a beautiful Spring day – that I got down into the town. I didn't know where I was supposed to walk to.' Corporal Joseph Bryan. 2 Welsh Guards attached 20 Guards Brigade Anti-Tank Company.[11]

Although 2 and 3 Companies had borne the brunt of the morning's attacks, 1 and 4 Companies on the left flank did not get off lightly either. Heavy fire from all types of weapon was directed on units of 4 Company.

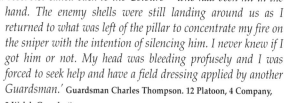

'*Slowly 12 Platoon and 4 Company were pushed back into the outskirts of the town, establishing from time to time points of resistance and getting some cover in or behind houses and other buildings which resulted in the Germans bringing heavier weapons and tank guns to bear on us, inevitably forcing us back again. We were suffering casualties and it was at one of these resistance points when I was firing at a sniper who was hiding behind the parapet on the top of a church tower...when I was blown from behind my protective pillar, one of several holding up the roof of a lean to building occupied by some of my platoon. I was struck by shrapnel on the right side of my face which took off part of my ear lobe before penetrating my head behind the upper cheek bone. Picking myself up I saw that most of the lean-to was a heap of rubble with no sign of my comrades except Guardsman Nichols – a reservist called back to the Colours – who had been hit in the hand. The enemy shells were still landing around us as I returned to what was left of the pillar to concentrate my fire on the sniper with the intention of silencing him. I never knew if I got him or not. My head was bleeding profusely and I was forced to seek help and have a field dressing applied by another Guardsman.'* Guardsman Charles Thompson. 12 Platoon, 4 Company, 2 Welsh Guards. [12]

**Second Lieutenant
Peter Hanbury**

Second Lieutenant Peter Hanbury had moved from his original position and set up his HQ in a house opposite the church in St. Martin on the '...crossroads where the road from St. Omer to Boulogne crossed the road from Calais in the north.' Like Thompson, Hanbury thought that a sniper, a Fifth Columnist perhaps, was ensconced in the tower of St. Martin church. Rumours and stories of the German Fifth Column were rife amongst the ranks of the Guards. There were stories of German motorcyclists being hidden in the backs of innocent looking furniture vans which drew up to roadblocks only for the back door to open and the motorcycle to roar off, its rider having had a good look at the British position. There were other stories of men dressed as priests carrying questionable documents and mysterious long, glass pipettes. All of these stories, due to the isolation of posts and the proximity of endless streams of refugees, not surprisingly, fuelled Allied fears that the Germans or German sympathisers, were atop every church tower and behind every window frame. Many of the fears were probably unfounded but there is no doubt that rough justice was meted out to some civilians suspected of assisting the Germans. It would appear, however, that there was some substance to Peter Hanbury's fears regarding the 'sniper in the tower' of the church in St. Martin.

'Parachutist/fifth-columnist? in church started sniping at us and put one through my trouser leg. I went up to the church to see if anyone was up the tower. I did not wish to upset the priest, so took off my tin hat, which he thought strange, so I put it back on again and started climbing the stairs. He dragged me down. I then understood there was s a fifth columnist or a parachutist up there. It seemed very unwise to go up a circular staircase as he only had to lob a grenade down...to deal with me. I returned to my platoon and ordered Bartlett and another guardsman to neutralise his fire with two Bren guns. They slowly shot the top off the tower, and said a rifle had been dropped from the tower. Whether they had killed the opposition or wounded him I do not know but he stopped firing. It now appeared obvious that No. 3 company were not in possession of their position. Jim Windsor-Lewis told me this company was wiped out. Eddie's road block was on fire, and it looked as though the tanks were rolling up the company from left to right. Message came from Jim that I was to retreat at once.' Second Lieutenant Peter Hanbury. OC 12 Platoon, 4 Company, 2 Welsh Guards.[13]

Hanbury went to tell Captain Heber-Percy that he was leaving 1 Company's flank unprotected but was told to ignore the message from 3 Company and 'stay put'. Captain Henry Coombe-Tennant then appeared and told Hanbury to move his platoon back into its old positions near the light railway to prevent the Germans getting behind them. On reaching the open they came under heavy fire: thirty rounds hitting the ground around them in quick succession blowing Hanbury up into the air, across the road and pitching him into an open sewer. At any second Hanbury could have been blown to pieces, but in an extraordinary twist of the psyche that perhaps only war can induce, the only thing which sprang to mind as he crouched in the sewer amid the inferno, was whether he could catch VD from the effluent!

After moving forward a little more Hanbury found five men of 3 Company under Corporal White retreating. Hanbury rallied them and pressed on towards the railway but met his CO, Captain Jack Higgon, coming the other way with four wounded men being carried on doors each held by four guardsmen. The whole party, twenty-seven men in all, then retired towards the junction near the church and expected heavy fire when they reached the open where Hanbury had been blown into the sewer. The Germans never fired a shot. On reaching the comparative safety of the junction Hanbury ordered his platoon to retire with him. As they made their way back towards town Hanbury talked to a seriously wounded sergeant from Ralph Pilcher's platoon who was also walking back with, '...one arm off and a bloody tourniquet round it.'

'He said this was a change from public duties in London. I was sitting beside him during an air-raid when he died. First time I had heard the rattle in someone's throat as they died.' Second Lieutenant Peter Hanbury. OC 12 Platoon, 4 Company, 2 Welsh Guards.[14]

Prior to Jack Higgon returning with the wounded men 11 Platoon had been in their original positions but the German attack was escalating and with the lack of communication and direct orders some of the men were becoming anxious.

'We were on our own, squatting near this house wondering what to do and shells coming over. Mid-morning it got so "hot" Sergeant Hendry sent a young guardsman to Captain Higgon and asked him what were we to do and his instructions were "last man, last round" That's what we were told to do. Sergeant Hendry said "bugger it we'll hang on a bit and make dash for it." So he sent the other two or three off and said "you go, Pritchard and me will follow you." So we were the last two to leave the back of this house and we made directly over the fields to Boulogne. I remember distinctly running over bare fields when we came down from St. Martin's and coming to the top of the town before you come down the big hill. We were under a privet hedge and it started to bloody rain. Oh hell! As boys playing at "Cowboys and Indians" well, you'd go home wouldn't you?! I was stuck under this ruddy hedge and I was watching "Jerry" cooking up his dinner in the field opposite. It was about mid-day and he was frying up with his tanks. They were cooking away; just lolling around. They were having the time of their lives, cooking away and walking about within eye distance. You could distinguish them quite easily. Later we picked up a Sergeant Sankey who was lying under a hedge with his arm broken. We helped him up and handed him over to somebody who took him back. We finished up on a hill at the top of Boulogne in a mansion just above the citadel on the left. We held that for a while and thought we'd get back to town. Guardsman Syd Pritchard. 11 Platoon, 4 Company, 2 Welsh Guards.[15]

'Inevitably we had to retreat again as casualties mounted, the Germans now had the advantage of being above us and were pushing us hard. A mixed number from my company, probably some from others, gathered near an old fortress type of building near what I believe was close to the town

centre and it was then that I realised I was wounded in the chest, shrapnel having entered through my small pack. Meeting up with my platoon Lieutenant again [Second Lieutenant Peter Hanbury] having lost him in the fighting, he saw that my wounds were serious and ordered me to hand over my rifle and ammunition before making my way to the coast to receive attention. I was very reluctant to do so having been trained that the rifle was my best friend and must be looked after and never parted with. With regret I left my Lieutenant and others behind to resist as best they could and headed for the coast and harbour by now not very far away, where I found a medical aid post and received fresh bandages and a cup of tea. With many others I waited to find transport to England.' Guardsman Charles Thompson. 12 Platoon, 4 Company, 2 Welsh Guards.[16]

The Germans were indeed above the Welsh and pushing hard. Early that morning they had captured Fort de la Creche and had reached the coast. *Oberleutnant* Durkes had woken up that morning and found himself staring up at the monumental la Colonne Napoléon, topped by the verdigris figure of the French Emperor himself. Durkes had climbed the 265 steps with *Oberst* von Vaerst for a commanding view of the whole of Boulogne and his objective that morning, Fort de la Creche. On the stroke of ten, German time, the German artillery had opened fire on the fort and the dismounted motorcyclists had ridden hell for leather down the 1000 metre slope to the railway on the back of the bucking panzers. In fifteen

German and French graves on Mont Lambert after the battle.
Courtesy Mairie de St Martin Boulogne

Above: The fall of Fort de la Creche. German motorcycle troops had left their machines to ride on the back of the panzers in an all out dash on the French position. Their boldness paid off. Here French prisoners are photographed with their German captors outside one of the recently captured bunkers.

Left: *Generaloberst* Heinz Guderian congratulates the men who took Fort de la Creche.

Courtesy Herr Franz Steinzer

minutes Durkes had got as far as the fort and was cutting away the protective wire. Minutes later the Germans had forced their way inside and were taking the French gunners prisoner as they came up out of their bunkers. The rest of the fort was then 'combed out' and the position consolidated. A troop of 2 Anti-Aircraft Regiment on the landward slopes behind the fort also had its guns knocked out after they had engaged two of the German tanks.

A little less than two kilometres away down the hill into Boulogne Colonel Deane's AMPC had been in position on the left of the Welsh since the early hours. On the extreme left flank, in advance of the Casino, the remnants of 5 Buffs commanded by Major Penlington supported by fifty AMPC personnel had been waiting astride the coast road. This mixed force had erected road-blocks using abandoned lorries and cars and the furniture from bombed out houses. The Germans had probed their positions shortly after they had got into position but had withdrawn only to return shortly afterwards with light tanks. With only rifle fire to defend themselves, the mixed force had watched the leading tank approach and climb the first barricade. As soon as the tank's nose had risen to an angle at which it could not fire its guns on the defenders the road block had been drenched with petrol and set alight, at which point the tank had reversed out of trouble. Under cover of the pall of smoke the Buffs and the AMPC had hurriedly constructed a new barricade but the attack had not been pressed. That said, the presence of German armour so close to the northern limits of the town and within striking distance of the port at that early hour was proof positive that the iron ring was closing around Boulgne. The final nail in the coffin was the capture of Fort de la Creche which dominated the northern land routes into the town and cut it off from the north. For the Welsh Guards once the fighting had started in earnest at 7.30 am there had been nowhere else to go except in the direction of the docks.

As *Oberleutnant* Durkes had savoured his moment of victory and the various edible 'luxuries' which his men had unearthed in the French bunkers after the battle for Fort de la Creche, he had looked down from his lofty perch and had seen two British destroyers enter the harbour and put to sea again after an hour. Durkes reflected that they had probably, 'evacuated the Tommies'. He had been wrong. All morning three British destroyers had stood off Boulogne repeatedly ignoring signals from Brigade HQ until around 11.00 am when one of them had nosed into the harbour and embarked a naval demolition party and a covering force of Royal Marines. It had sailed again shortly afterwards taking with it a situation report from Brigadier Fox-Pitt. The Welsh Guards were being hit hard and some of the more advanced companies of the Irish Guards on the other side of the Liane were also taking a beating as a result of heavy and persistent German attacks. With Boulogne effectively surrounded by a much stronger and better equipped foe it was not unreasonable to assume, as indeed had *Oberleutnant* Durkes, that the War Office would sanction the immediate evacuation of the entire Allied garrison given that the docks were still in Allied hands. A little later Fox-Pitt had received his instructions. All personnel of 'no military value' were indeed to be evacuated. The remainder of the force were to 'stand fast' and 'fight it out.'

By around 11.30 am the Welsh had held the Germans off for some four hours but in spite of poor communications it was becoming clear to Lieutenant Colonel Stanier that the pressure was beginning to tell. Captain Hodgkinson of HQ Company arrived at Battalion HQ to inform him that his position in front of Ostrohove was in danger of being enveloped and in view of the continued attacks on 2 and 3 Companies he decided to shorten his line. First, all HQ personnel and some sixty men of Colonel Deane's AMPC were pushed out as a screen facing northeast to defend battalion HQ. Stanier's plans involved 2 Company withdrawing to hold the houses facing south-east along the line of the light railway between the little halt in Ostrohove and Brequerecque. HQ and 3 Company would continue the line and link up with 4 and 1 Companies on the left at St. Martin. Before Stanier could send out messengers to his company commanders, however, he received orders from Brigadier Fox-Pitt to withdraw into Boulogne itself and block all approaches to the harbour from the AMPC blocks near the Casino along the banks of the River Liane as far as the main railway bridge. In the Haute Ville Major Windsor-Lewis received a message from Brigade to the effect that '...all Coys were withdrawing and to conform to this withdrawal to the quay.' Major Windsor-Lewis moved further downhill towards the Ville Bass and opted to defend a large, white building at the junction of the Rue du Mont St. Adrien and the present day Rue des Victoires. He told two sections to barricade the doors and windows while another section held a road block down the Rue Thiers to their right.

> *'In the afternoon I was ordered to establish road blocks in the town. Boulogne was to be held. I had few men left by this time, but with three sections forward covering road blocks and Coy. HQ down the street about 300 yds in rear, I took up position.'* Major J C Windsor-Lewis. OC 3 Company, 2 Welsh Guards.[17]

As it got under way the withdrawal was beset with difficulties. Effective communications were virtually impossible given the distances involved and the fact that most of the signalling equipment had been left on the quay after landing and had never found its way to the battalion. Every man Stanier had sent down to the quay to retrieve it had been hustled on board a waiting ship by over zealous embarkation officers. Stanier had used dispatch riders on commandeered French machines to ferry his messages around but it was a dangerous business given the sniping and shelling. By the end of the day the only man left able to ride a motorcycle would be

The port in flames. Photograph taken 24 May 1940, from the top of the Rue de Calais. Courtesy Mairie de St Martin Boulogne

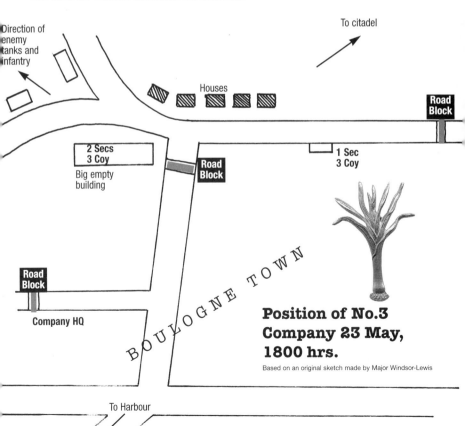

To citadel

Direction of enemy tanks and infantry

Houses

Road Block

2 Secs
3 Coy

Big empty building

Road Block

1 Sec
3 Coy

Road Block

Company HQ

BOULOGNE TOWN

Position of No.3 Company 23 May, 1800 hrs.

Based on an original sketch made by Major Windsor-Lewis

To Harbour

The Pont Marguet Bridge. Lieutenant Colonel Stanier set up his HQ in one of the hotels on the opposite side after the withdrawal from positions on the outer perimter.

Guardsman Potter. Only one line had been laid on the whole battalion front early that morning and that had been to Hexie Hughes's position, a position which no longer existed. This lack of communication was already leading to some men, like those in Syd Pritchard's section, being ordered to retire by their section commanders and it was to have further disastrous consequences for the men with Major Windsor-Lewis and men like Pritchard and Doug Davies now making their way back from the most advanced posts of the Welsh line without firm orders.

By about 2.00 pm the Battalion, with 4 Company acting as rearguard, had withdrawn under great difficulty to a line of posts running roughly north-south 500 metres from the quays, with their backs to the River Liane and facing east. Here they joined French troops and, as the remnants of 3 Company had already done, blocked the main roads leading to the harbour in order to delay the German advance by pushing them into narrow alleys and side streets. Lieutenant Colonel Stanier chose, as his battalion HQ, a hotel down by the quay, near to the Pont Marguet bridge.

'It was called Hotel de la Paix. Wasn't much "de la Paix" about it...there I was overrun by Colonels and people saying "What am I to do? I've got a battalion can I help you?" Of course they were the most awful nuisance poor things, and I was terribly sorry for them. There were some very gallant old soldiers there and they were put in the bag, spent the war in prison.
Lieutenant Colonel Sir Alexander Stanier Bt., MC. CO 2 Welsh Guards.[18]

The Welsh were now being fired on from houses on both banks of the Liane as the Germans took advantage of the pronounced eastward kink in the river's course and pushed onto the neck of land on the opposite bank in rear of 2 Company. To add to the Guards' problems, shots were coming from the direction of Brigade HQ which had been set up near the Gare Maritime, as AMPC personnel and inexperienced, leaderless troops still armed with rifles, shot at anything that moved – friend or foe – on the opposite bank. Fire was also being directed on Colonel Deane's AMPC posts at the road blocks near the Casino so he drove across the Pont Marguet to enlist Brigadier Fox-Pitt's support in putting a stop to the indiscriminate firing. As Deane crossed the bridge the engine of his car was riddled by machine-gun fire but he made it across. The Brigadier promised to do all he could but was unsure whether the few guardsmen at Brigade HQ could successfully bring such a large body of obviously nervous men under control. Deane re-crossed the bridge on foot and returned to his command. A little later Billy Fox-Pitt went to see Alexander Stanier at the Hotel de la Paix just as Stanier was returning from personally redistributing the Battalion in company areas. It was the first time Fox-Pitt had seen his old 1st Battalion comrade since their meeting at St. Martin

A self-propelled heavy infantry gun, 15cm, mounted on a 1 Ausf B tank chassis, on the approaches to Boulogne during the fighting.

earlier that morning and the first opportunity he had had to pass on his orders from the War Office. In spite of the German pressure from all sides he informed Stanier that the Guards would still have to 'fight it out'. Boulogne was to be held.

1. Guardsman Charles Thompson. 12 Platoon, 4 Company, 2 Welsh Guards. Account sent to author.
2. Guardsman Syd Pritchard. 11 Platoon, 4 Company, 2 Welsh Guards. Author's tape transcript.
3. Guardsman Arthur Boswell. 8 Platoon, 3 Company, 2 Welsh Guards. Account sent to author.
4. Lieutenant Colonel Sir Alexander Stanier Bt., MC. CO 2 Welsh Guards. *Gort's Army – The British Expeditionary Force of 1939-1940*. IWM Sound Archive – 7175/7.
5. Corporal Joseph Bryan. 2 Welsh Guards attached 20 Guards Brigade Anti-Tank Company. Author's tape transcript.
6. Lieutenant Colonel Sir Alexander Stanier Bt., MC. CO 2 Welsh Guards. *op.cit.*
7. Lieutenant Colonel Sir Alexander Stanier Bt., MC. CO 2 Welsh Guards. *ibid.*
8. Major J C Windsor-Lewis OC 3 Company, 2 Welsh Guards. PRO CAB 106/228.
9. Guardsman Arthur Boswell. *op.cit.*
10. Guardsman Doug Davies. 8 Platoon, 3 Company, 2 Welsh Guards. Author's tape transcript.
11. Corporal Joseph Bryan. *op.cit.*
12. Guardsman Charles Thompson. *op.cit.*
13. Second Lieutenant Peter Hanbury. OC 12 Platoon, 4 Company, 2 Welsh Guards. *A Not Very Military Experience.*
14. *ibid*
15. Guardsman Syd Pritchard. *op.cit.*
16. Guardsman Charles Thompson. *op.cit.*
17. Major J C Windsor-Lewis. *op.cit.*
18. Lieutenant Colonel Sir Alexander Stanier Bt., MC. CO 2 Welsh Guards. *op.cit.*

Chapter 7

'ALL TALL FELLOWS'

The German assault on the Irish Guards line, which began at 7.30 am on 23 May, initially fell on 1 Company as it had the previous day. Panzers began to advance along the low road through Outreau which had been opened the night before with the destruction of the Irish anti-tank guns. *Oberleutnant* Künzel watched the tanks and rifle companies advance as he and his men took advantage of a days rest from the fighting. As they rested they witnessed the first of the prisoners being marched out of Boulogne as the Germans combed out the southern suburbs.

> *'At the double they arrive, all races: Frenchmen, Belgians, Dutchmen, Negroes from the Belgian Congo...Algerians, Moroccans – and Englishmen...the Englishmen show proud, dogged faces. Now they are marching 'to Berlin' but as prisoners! Among the uninterrupted streaming columns...there are too, the 'Englishmen' who had manned the anti-tank gun position, all tall fellows. Irish Guards as we learn. They had behaved tough.'* Oberleutnant **Künzel** [1]

Instead of pressing their assault against 1 Company as they had done the previous day the Germans quickly switched the point of attack to Captain Murphy's 4 Company, concentrating particularly on the forward platoon led by Lieutenant Peter Reynolds, dug in near the reservoir and trigonometrical point at la Tour de Renard. Reynolds' platoon held a hump of high ground which fell away on both flanks and to their rear. From the summit of the hump a track ran due south-west across level ground and dipped after some 600 metres just before meeting another track coming uphill from Manihen. Beyond the reservoir were patches of 'dead ground'

French colonial troops being rounded up by the Germans in the town suburbs.

Lieutenant Peter Reynolds. Killed in action 23 May 1940.

Courtesy Sir John Leslie

and there were many hidden folds and hollows to the south-west which could conceal approaching armour. Reynolds' position was not an envious one. The loss of 1 Company's forward platoon and the destruction of the anti-tank guns to his left the night before had left him somewhat exposed, particularly as there were large gaps between him and the platoon under Second Lieutenant Jack Leslie dug in near the farm at the road junction 300 metres or so to his right rear. Here, in places where the ground fell away from the summit to the west, some of Jack Leslie's posts were below the level of the surrounding hills.

'Peter Reynolds was to my left but we had lost contact with his platoon as we were stretched too thinly.'[2] Second Lieutenant Jack Leslie, 4 Company, 2 Irish Guards

The Germans began by shelling Reynolds with guns and mortars and then lifted their fire to concentrate on the rest of the battalion front. As the guns lifted the tanks moved in to isolate the platoon. With no supporting arms the Irish Guards fought armour with rifle bullets for more than an hour but it was only a matter of time before the panzers, realising the lack of Irish firepower, seized their chance to drive straight over and through the guardsmen. At this point Lieutenant Simon Leveson appeared on foot with the leading section of his carrier platoon to reinforce Reynolds. Leveson had been ordered forward from the centre of Outreau to reinforce 1 Company but as he advanced he came to the conclusion that Reynolds was in need of more help than 1 Company at that time. With his leading section he moved towards the pocket being so valiantly defended by Peter Reynolds and his men.

'Simon Leveson came walking up with his platoon in single file. At that time there was a lull in the firing and Simon told me that a German attack was imminent. He took his men and an anti-tank gun he had up to the platoon at the top of the hill and got killed there.'[3]

Second Lieutenant Jack Leslie, 4 Company, 2 Irish Guards

By 8.45 am the situation around la Tour de Renard had become so grave that the only option left to Captain Murphy was to withdraw Reynolds' men quickly if they were to be saved at all. Lieutenant Colonel Haydon agreed but by then it was already too late. The German noose had tightened and Reynolds and Leveson were surrounded. Captain Murphy and Captain Reid tried desperately to reach them but each time they did so the torrent of fire sweeping the hillsides beat them back. There was no doubt in Captain Murphy's mind that no-one could have got through to Reynolds' platoon alive.

'The German tanks came up from a direction we weren't expecting. They came up from the direction of the railway. They had obviously curved

around our flank. Shells from our own destroyers began to land on the road ahead of us as they tried to break up the German advance.'[4]

Second Lieutenant Jack Leslie, 4 Company, 2 Irish Guards

Both Peter Reynolds and Simon Leveson were killed in action whilst Second Lieutenant Jack Leslie and the wounded Lieutenant Pat Butler, were captured.

'There were bullets flashing all around us in our trenches and a lot of noise – people were shouting at the tops of their voices and the next thing we knew a German sergeant appeared some yards off wielding a stick grenade shouting, "Aus, Aus, Aus." There was nothing for it but to get out of our trench. If we hadn't he would have blown us all to pieces. We had to run about 200-300 yards back towards the German positions near the reservoir where they lined us up as the battle moved on. Later all the wounded were treated along with the German wounded and we spent the night in the field there before we were marched off towards Montreuil.'[5]

Lieutenant Hugh Simon Leveson Killed in action 23 May 1940.
Courtesy Sir John Leslie

Second Lieutenant Jack Leslie, 4 Company, 2 Irish Guards

Only nineteen men of 4 Company would answer their names during roll call on their eventual return to England out of 107 other ranks who left Dover for Boulogne on 22 May.

Now that the Germans had destroyed the forward platoons of both 1 and 4 Companies it was perhaps inevitable that Lieutenant Colonel Haydon began to think in terms of readjusting his line. At 9.00 am Captain McCausland collected his remaining men and withdrew to the centre of Outreau where they covered the road leading down the hill into Boulogne and the road leading to Battalion HQ around the point where the railway disappeared into the Tunnel de l'Ave Maria which ran for almost two kilometres beneath Outreau towards the coast on it way to the southern quays of the harbour. Haydon visited Captain Murphy at 4 Company HQ fifteen minutes later and ordered him to pull his left flank back to join hands with 1 Company. He then ordered Captain Madden to send a platoon of 2 Company to stiffen the left flank of Murphy's depleted command. Such was the pressure being brought to bear on 4 Company however, that forty-five minutes later Murphy was forced to withdraw again from the southern outskirts of Outreau to positions on the left of 1 Company which approximated the line of the railway tunnel on the few maps Lieutenant Colonel Haydon possessed. 2 Company pulled its left flank back to conform whilst the men of 3 Company, as yet unmolested, remained in their original positions astride the coast road near Le Portel. Lieutenant Colonel Haydon sent Major Ross, his second in command, further back down the hill towards Boulogne to reconnoitre a new and shortened line of defence. His original intention was to hold the line with three companies, keeping 2 Company in reserve but the intention was

RECOMMENDATIONS.

No 1 Coy   2nd Bn Irish Guards.

Gdsn Montgomery.   ⓒ

This Guardsman was a member of L/cpl Mawhinney's Section, and when this Section was cut off by the enemy he was of the utmost assistance to his Section Comdr both acting as Scout and covering the withdrawal of the Section with a Bren Gun.
      At this time an Enemy Tank was within 30 yards of the Section post.
      Later this man used a Bren gun with great effect, at a road junction in the village of Outreau, and was instrumental in inflicting considerable casualties on the enemy which delayed his advance to no small extent.
      All through the day he was to be seen in the thick of the fight, behind a Bren gun, a rifle or an A.T. Rifle. He was one of an escort to his Commanding Officer on an exceedingly difficult and dangerous reconnaissance through the streets and purlieus of Boulogne and appeared absolutely tireless in the execution of his duty. In my opinion Gdsn. Montgomery showed a magnificent example of fearlessness, and coolness, and untiring energy in all the many activities and Battles of that day.

C R Mawland Captain.
Comdg, No 1 Coy.
2nd Bn. Irish Guards.

never realised. He had not at that stage appreciated the fact that, '...1 and 4 Companies had already been reduced to almost microscopic numbers.'

Just as a light railway had run through the rear of the Welsh line, so one ran behind the Irish. From its furthest extremity in Le Portel the line ran due north-east towards the Liane for approximately one kilometre before taking a long, slow left hand curve down the hill towards the docks, a further 1,250 metres distant. The section of the railway as it ran downhill just after the left hand curve, formed part of the new line selected by Major Ross from which the battalion could cover the western and southern approaches to Boulogne on the west bank of the Liane. The Irish began the withdrawal to their new positions in gardens and houses astride the light railway at around 10.30 am and the bulk of the battalion was in position an hour later, minus 3 and 1 Companies. 3 Company, which had thus far escaped face-to-face contact with the Germans on the right flank, later withdrew without molestation to conform to the new line. 1 Company on the other hand were at that time still heavily engaged by German troops who had dogged their withdrawal every step of the way into Outreau The guardsmen had been exchanging fire with groups of Germans at ranges of between thirty and fifty metres since before 9.45 am and had beaten off every attempt to outflank them. Captain McCausland finally extricated his remaining men and moved down towards the light railway where he joined the rest of the battalion at 11.45 am. It was a superb example of discipline under fire taking into account the heavy and repeated attacks the company had endured the previous day and the resultant casualties. Excluding his officers, McCausland had landed with 100 men under his command. Only forty would manage to get back home and most of the sixty who would later be posted as killed, wounded or missing were already lost. It was a credit to all ranks that they were able to disengage without further heavy loss of life. Captain Mc Causland's personal example of leadership in holding a key post throughout this dangerous phase of the withdrawal was later recognised with the award of the Distinguished Service Order.

As the Irish fell back the Germans followed up, creeping cautiously into street after street until they made contact with the Irish rearguard and then trying to slip across the railway to penetrate the streets behind them. Prodigious quantities of ammunition were expended sweeping the ends of streets with fire in an attempt to prevent German infiltration.

In a garage to the side of the railway line Lieutenant H R Grace of the Royal Army Medical Corps had set up his Regimental Aid Post (RAP) and was tending a steady stream of wounded with the assistance of Father Julian Stoner, the Chaplain. Inside the dimly lit garage the noise of battle roared incessantly, the heavy thud of exploding shells seeming to creep closer every second. Father Stoner, poking his head out into the daylight to see what was happening, expected to see the streets littered with corpses but the only man he saw was Lieutenant Patrick Davison standing behind a wall with a revolver in his hand. The din of rifle and machine-gun fire indicated that there were hundreds of men, both Irish Guards and Germans, all around him but Father Stoner saw no other living soul; they were too well hidden.

During the two hours or so that the Guards made their stand astride the light railway they were fighting almost continuously, so much so that when Lieutenant Colonel Haydon ordered a further retirement towards the docks at around 1.00pm, and the Irish began to fall back once more towards the quays, some of the Bren guns had to be left behind as the barrels had warped due to the heat or they had become clogged with dirt.

They moved off in a long column down a 'fairly important street' with the head and tail protected by Bren guns and anti-tank rifles. Using the line of the railway as a target the Germans then began to shell the surrounding streets and the Irish scuttled into the houses on either side of their line of retirement to prevent unnecessary casualties. Bren gunners and men armed with Boys anti-tank rifles sealed off the roads in which the companies were sheltering. Officers and NCOs sheltered in the doorways ready to bring the men out as soon as the 'all clear' order was given but almost as soon as it had started the shelling ceased. Before the men could move on they heard, in the deathly silence which followed the shelling, the ominous rattle of tank tracks moving slowly towards them along the cobbled streets. With hearts in their mouths the men watched as five German tanks lumbered slowly towards them preceded by a man in civilian clothes gesticulating wildly and proclaiming that the tanks were French. The man and the three leading tanks continued down the hill but two remained in the street; one of them outside a house in which a sergeant and his section were sheltering and the other outside the house next door being used by staff of Battalion HQ. Major D J L Fitzgerald's *History of the Irish Guards in the Second World War* records what happened next as the guardsmen lay crouched on the floor inside the houses and stole anxious glances into the street.

> *'The sergeant was wondering what he could do, when a civilian walked in the back door. The stranger quickly unbuttoned his mackintosh to show a French uniform, pointed to the front door and said "Francais". The sergeant opened the door cautiously to have a look at the tank which was noisily turning around. The "French" officer fled out of the back door, and 'taking time from him' the section flung themselves on their faces just as the tanks shots rocketed down the passage.'*

Next door, Lieutenant J Marnon the Signals Officer, was fretting as he knew he had left a motorcycle propped up against the wall outside but the tank did little more than spray a window or doorway with machine-gun fire every now and then. The Irish felt trapped. They were, in the words of Lieutenant Colonel Haydon '...in the most difficult and perilous situation.' How long would the tanks wait? Would the Germans start to search the houses? The minutes dragged by but within a quarter of an hour all questions were answered when the three tanks that had gone down the hill returned to join the two parked in the street and all five withdrew once more the way they had come. Haydon could not now be certain that the

Troops of 2 Panzer Division move cautiously down a suburban street. Courtesy Herr Fritz Steinzer

way to the quay was clear. More tanks may have moved down other streets whilst the battalion had been trapped inside the houses and so he sent a patrol down towards the quay to make sure. The patrol reached its destination and met Lieutenant Sir John Reynolds who was the battalion liaison officer attached to 20 Guards Brigade. He told them that there had been no sign of German tanks in the vicinity of the dockside. Whilst the patrol was away Lieutenant J D Hornung the intelligence officer, saw two 'very small' tanks sweep up the street through the battalion area. A guardsman managed to get off quick a shot with an anti-tank rifle and scored a direct hit on the rear of one of the tanks, but as small as the tank was the shot appeared to make 'no impression whatsoever.'

It was by now around 3pm and at Brigade HQ Brigadier Fox-Pitt thought he perceived a distinct lull in the firing. It seemed possible that the Germans had withdrawn from their forward positions and an officer sent out towards the Haute Ville found that the Germans had indeed withdrawn, a move which aroused suspicion on the part of the Brigadier in view of German persistence during the morning's fighting. The entry in Guderian's *XIX Korps* War Diary for 14.45 hours goes some way to explaining the reasoning behind the German pause. Guderian and his staff were under the impression that,

> *'... in and around Boulogne the enemy is fighting tenaciously for every inch of ground in order to prevent the harbour from falling into German hands.* Luftwaffe *attacks on warships and transports lying off Boulogne are inadequate: it is not clear whether the latter are engaged in embarkation or disembarkation. 2nd Arrmoured Division's attack therefore only progresses slowly.'*

The battle was not going as smoothly as the Germans had planned and

111

amongst the men on the ground there was a whiff of uncertainty and confusion in the air.

'The Command knows the difficulty of the task. A coup de main by the right Combat Group [Vaerst] does not succeed until the second attempt. Enemy air attack at Mont Lambert claims victims. Cruisers, destroyers and torpedo boats, altogether eight warships outside the harbour, again and again lay well-aimed fire on the attackers. At Wimereux, le Portel and at the aerodrome south of Boulogne, English troops are disembarking according to reports from reconnaissance planes. Hostile tank forces are reported marching from Calais to Boulogne, from Bazinhem marching enemy columns are approaching. Again and again units are to be detached to parry them off. In vain the artillery tries to combat the destroyers at sea. The range (of the artillery) does not suffice. The absence of III Rifle Battalion still waiting for relief on the Somme sector, becomes even more conspicuous. About 16.00 hours [German time] the attack breaks down under the well-aimed fire of the destroyers. Last night we could have done without your pleasure but now-come on comrades of the Luftwaffe.'[6]   Oberleutnant **Dietz**.

A flotilla of Allied warships were still lying off Boulogne, several of the World War One vintage 'V and W' Class destroyers like HMS *Vimy* and HMS *Whitshed* were amongst them, as was *L'Orage* and several more French ships, described by Don Harris aboard the *Vimy* as 'the most modern of the world's destroyers.' Guderian requested an attack on the harbour to disrupt the movement of ships in and out of the port and so put an end to any threat of landing further fighting units. The *Luftwaffe* did not respond in force immediately to Guderian's request but nevertheless sporadic raids by Stukas on the harbour area were a constant threat.

Uncertain of the Germans' next move Fox-Pitt used the lull to send his own message to his battalions. Still waiting for news from his own patrol as to whether the streets were clear of German armour, Lieutenant Colonel Haydon was unsure as to whether his battalion was to be evacuated or not but a dispatch rider who arrived some minutes later seemed to provide a glimmer of hope. The message, timed at 15.05 hours, was sent as 'written' from Brigade HQ to both 2 Irish and 2 Welsh Guards.

'20 Gds Bde and details will embark as under as accommodation arises

HMS *Whitshed*.

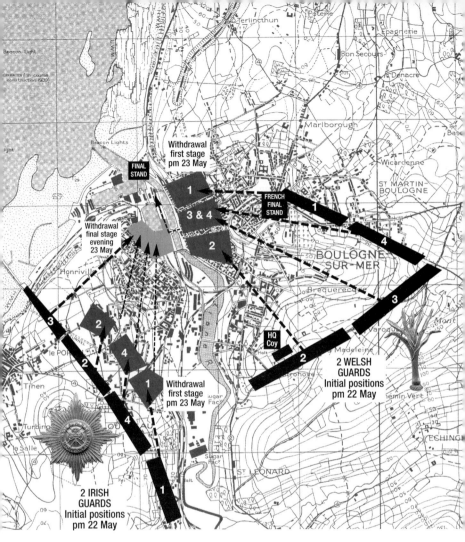

STOP All AMPC and non combatant units in WITSHED (sic) and non combatant and stragglers not under comd Bns as accommodation becomes available STOP 2 Irish and 2 Welsh Gds will hold bridgehead as at present STOP These two Bns will withdraw under direct orders of Brigadier in order 2 Welsh 2 Irish.'[7]

As soon as the patrol came back with word that the quaysides on the west of the harbour were clear, Lieutenant Colonel Haydon issued orders for the final move to the docks. Led by an advance guard ready to drop Brens and anti-tank rifles at any side roads which might have to be held, and with a rear-guard protecting its back, the battalion moved off. Sergeant William Gilchrist was one of the men who had been protecting the battalion's 'tail' during the withdrawal most of the afternoon. With a small party of men he had held a post at a street corner with an anti-tank rifle for the better part of two hours under heavy machine-gun fire. On another street corner not far away Lance Corporal Ivan Burke was also part of the rearguard. He had succeeded in holding off the Germans by operating both a Bren gun and an anti-tank rifle until he had collapsed, partly due to exhaustion and partly due to concussion from a shell landing close by. Both men would later receive recognition for their actions during the bitter street fighting that day; Gilchrist with the award of the Distinguished Conduct Medal and Burke the Military Medal.

It took the battalion the best part of an hour to move the last 800 metres or so down to the quayside due to a diversion to avoid sniping from an upstairs window in a side street. When they finally reached the area on the western quays of the Bassin Napoléon at around 4pm the Irish barricaded all the approach roads with vehicles and barrels and set up posts to cover them with automatic weapons whilst the majority took cover inside sheds and warehouses. Some of the men headed for a quayside café but Drill-Sergeant Kelly was already there standing sentinel over the rows of coloured bottles behind the bar. According to Kelly the liquid inside the bottles was 'poisoned' and none of the men dared touched a drop. A little later, however, the battalion was ordered out of the sheds and warehouses to defend the roads into the harbour from the west and south. The hope of evacuation for 20 Brigade appeared to be evaporating. Now, with all the surrounding high ground in German hands, there was little else that Brigadier Fox-Pitt could do but hold the port and buy precious time for the Royal Navy as it began the hazardous task of evacuating the many hundreds of civilian evacuees, BEF wounded and stragglers, non combatants and raw French, Belgian and Dutch soldiery from under the noses of the advancing Germans. The harbour area had been under accurate, close range artillery and mortar fire for some time and now, despite the lull at around 3 pm, small arms fire was beginning to rake the sheds and warehouses in the vicinity of the fish market and along the quays around the Bassin Napoléon as German infantry seeped into the surrounding streets. Just beyond the breakwaters HMS *Whitshed* was steaming towards the harbour and making ready to come alongside.

1. *Oberleutnant* Künzel. Einnahme von Boulogne-sur-Mer, in Militär-Wochenblatt, No.35, Cols. 1517-1521. (Berlin 1940)

2. Second Lieutenant Jack Leslie. Conversation with author.

3. *ibid*

4. *ibid*

5. *ibid*

6. *Oberleutnant* Dietz. Abbeville und Boulogne unter den Schlagen einer Panzerdivision in Guderian Generaloberst H (Ed) Mit den Panzern in Ost und West. Vol. 1.

7. IWM Department of Documents – 93/28/24

CHAPTER EIGHT

THE SCRAP IRON FLOTILLA

HMS *Whitshed* had recently escorted 20 Brigade across the Channel and indeed had carried Brigadier Fox-Pitt and his HQ staff to Boulogne but her association with the Irish Guards went back even further than that. It was the *Whitshed* which had evacuated the Headquarters Company of the composite battalion of Irish and Welsh Guards – 'Harpoon Force' – from the Hook of Holland a week earlier on 14 May. On that occasion the Irish had won the approval of the *Whitshed's* officers for their discipline.

Now the *Whitshed* was to be associated with the Irish Guards for the third time that month. As she came alongside the Quai Chanzy and cleared a long shed near the Gare Maritime the naval officers on her bridge heard machine-gun fire which sounded very close indeed. One of those officers later wrote an account of what he saw that afternoon in *Blackwood's Magazine*, quoted in the *History of the Irish Guards in the Second World War*.

> '*A section of Irish Guards were engaging with rifle fire an enemy machine-gun post established in a warehouse, as coolly and methodically as if they had been on the practice ranges. "Tell the foremost guns to open fire", the Captain yelled. The guns swung round and with a crash two 4.7 HE shells tore into the building and blew it to the skies. Meanwhile as the German infantry now passed ahead of their tanks and infiltrated closer and closer to the quays, the fine discipline of the Guards earned the awed, open-mouthed respect of all. Watching them in perfect order, moving exactly together, engaging target after target as though on parade ground drill, it was difficult to realise that this was the grim reality of battle. They were truly magnificent and no sailor who saw them could ever forget the feeling of pride he experienced.*'

Naval landing parties went ashore and joined the Irish in defending the streets around the harbour whilst the embarkation of refugees, wounded soldiers, stragglers and AMPC personnel got under way. When she had loaded as many troops and refugees as possible the *Whitshed* put to sea bound for Dover and almost as soon as she had cleared the harbour HMS *Keith* and HMS *Vimy* began their approach. Lieutenant G J A Lumsden was the navigator on board the *Keith*.

> '*As we entered harbour we passed a number of British and French destroyers bombarding the aerodrome, [at Cap d'Alprech] which was in German hands. Boulogne harbour is approached by a narrow channel between long stone piers with a kink to the right in the channel just before it enters the harbour proper: there is a small spinney to the left there and the*

close-packed town rises up the hillside to about 150 feet behind it and along the road lining the quay. We secured at the railway quay to starboard with Vimy outside us...The General commanding troops came aboard so that he could report a desperate situation to the War Office in London: he was ordered to hold the port to the last man. We could see a few of our soldiers in the spinney on the other side of the harbour and lying in the streets with Bren guns but the considerable number of Pioneer Corps men and fearful civilians on the quay alongside us were not so impressive. We embarked any wounded but no one else at this stage. Fifty years later our RNVR Midshipman told me that he had been ordered to find the Naval Officer in charge ashore; armed with a pistol he walked up the quay and round a building to find himself facing a German tank.' Lieutenant G J A Lumsden. RN.'

Don Harris was aboard the *Vimy* and was proud of her service record. She was a 'V and W' class destroyer like the *Whitshed*, having been launched in 1917 and, along with other ships of the same class, had served in the latter stages of the First World War. The *Vimy* had sailed on into the Second World War with performances which, in Harris's eyes, upheld a glorious tradition and gave the lie to the rather ungracious tag of her being part of the 'scrap iron flotilla'. He too saw French ships of their 2nd Destroyer Flotilla under the command of *Capitaine* Urvoy Porzamparc firing on the advancing Germans.

'On arrival we could clearly see large numbers of German Army

HMS *Vimy*.

116

Spotting for the German artillery – the Fieseler *Storch*.

Don Harris of HMS *Vimy*.
Courtesy Mr R Summers

advance units swarming down the high ground approaches leading to the city. They were being bombarded from offshore by four French destroyers. We signalled a request for one or two to accompany us into the port to evacuate troops, UK and French, plus numerous female nursing staff. The reply was a definite refusal, "no, it is suicidal to go in there, we will continue to bombard." And so we proceeded into the narrow harbour...The wharf and railway station on our starboard side was packed with those hopeful of being evacuated. On our port side and in close proximity were hotels and various other business establishments. The advance German Army units were beginning to pick up our range and soon casualties from their light calibre shells were mounting at an alarming rate.'* Don Harris[2]

About an hour after the ships had berthed Lieutenant Lumsden looked up to see a Fieseler *Storch* reconnaissance plane flying slowly over the harbour. He told his Captain it meant trouble. A little later, at around 6.00pm, word came through that the War Office had changed its policy. In spite of the fact that General Lanquetot's force was still intact and holding out behind the thick medieval

117

ramparts of the Haute Ville, the British Government came to the unilateral conclusion that Boulogne was no longer defensible and the order for complete evacuation was passed on to Brigadier Fox-Pitt. Winston Churchill later conceded that he agreed to the evacuation of Boulogne 'with reluctance'. The French government were not consulted and neither was General Lanquetot, nor would he receive any notice of British intentions. Indeed, the decision to evacuate merely added leverage to a rift in the French Government and armed forces and fanned the flames of anti-British sentiment amongst the *mous*, the 'doves', who had rallied behind Marshal Pétain and who were sceptical about the true value of Britain as an ally. In the eyes of Pétain's anglophobic supporters the British were less than keen in their desire to fight the Germans to the last. The evacuation order had one further consequence. When the time came, a few days later, to decide on the fate of the British garrison in Calais, Churchill would recall the Boulogne decision. For the, 'sake of Allied solidarity' he would rule that there would be no evacuation from Calais. There, they would fight to the finish.

At Boulogne however, with the decision to evacuate made, Fox-Pitt was informed that destroyers would be sent in to take off the Guards. The race was now on. The Germans were closing in and his battalions could not hold out for very much longer without artillery support, air cover or effective anti-tank weapons but the quays were still thronged with people. The Brigadier decided that his battalions should hold their present line until the logjam on the quays could be thinned out. He hurriedly composed a message to be sent out to Lieutenant Colonels Stanier and Haydon.

'Bde will evacuate BOULOGNE forthwith STOP All personnel of non-combatant units and other units now on quay will be evacuated first STOP 2 Irish Gds and 2 Welsh Gds will withdraw at Zero hour to be issued later STOP All HQ and reserves start withdrawing Zero-40 STOP Posns may be thinned out at Zero-30 STOP Posn to be finally abandoned at Zero STOP All ranks will embark on any destroyer available on arrival at quay. Time of origin 18.32.'[3]

He was on the point of sending the message out when the Luftwaffe, which had been bombing the harbour intermittently all day, struck in force in response to Guderian's earlier plea. The German troops on the ground were overjoyed.

'The officers are lying behind their scissors telescopes and observe the manoeuvres of the warships Again and again they look back and search the horizon in vain. Then, a look at the watch – 19.30 hours – a slight wail of sirens in a few minutes swelling to an ear deafening noise. Scarcely perceivable they soar above the ships like a dark cloud bringing death and ruin. The first, the second, the third – the eyes cannot follow the individual

The message from Brigadier Fox-Pitt to Lieutenant Colonel Haydon ordering the evacuation. Courtesy the estate of Miss Malise Haydon

> *planes – dive through the dots of AA shell explosions down on their victims. Detonations, flashes, huge fountains, din of engines and away they go.'*
> Oberleutnant Dietz.[1]

Estimates of the number of planes involved vary but several accounts refer to a figure of between eighty and ninety machines involved in the raid. Lieutenant Lumsden was on the bridge of the *Keith* with his Captain, forty-seven year old David 'Ginger' Simson, a vastly experienced destroyer officer who was also in command of 19 Destroyer Flotilla. At home in England, Simson's wife Arlette was ill in bed with chickenpox. In spite of this he had deliberately kissed her goodbye before leaving for this latest tour of duty. They had been married for just six months.

From the bridge Lumsden and Simson were observing the progress of people down the gangways and ladders leading to the Flag Deck below them, when Lumsden heard the unmistakable drone of approaching aircraft.

> *'We heard and sighted a large force of aircraft approaching from the north-east, there were two forces of 30 Stuka dive-bombers each and a third force of 30 twin-engined bombers. The 30 twin-engined aircraft moved in to attack the area of the town which our soldiers held on the north side of the harbour opposite us and about 100 yards distant. To our astonishment just as they began to drop their bombs twelve RAF Spitfire fighters appeared from England and attacked them head-on, completely breaking up their attack. One squadron of 30 Stukas proceeded to attack the destroyers*

Stukas – the scourge of the Allied destroyers.

outside the harbour sinking a French and damaging a British destroyer. The remaining 30 Stukas in single line wheeled to a point about 2,000 feet above us and close to the south-west, and then poured down in a single stream to attack the crowded quay and our two destroyers. The only opposition to this...was scattered rifle fire...mostly from soldiers ashore and the single barrelled two-pounder pom-poms in each destroyer...As the attack began, with immediate and terrible effect on the quay, the Captain ordered bridge people below because the bridge was just above quay-level and therefore exposed to splinters from bombs bursting there. Finally he decided that, as we could do nothing useful, he and I would leave the bridge. I stood back to allow him down the bridge ladder to the wheelhouse, as courtesy and seniority demanded, but he signed me to precede him: no Captain likes to leave his bridge when under attack. I had taken one or two steps down when, alas, he fell down on top of me, shot in the chest by a German sniper's bullet: it must have passed close to my head. We laid our Captain on the settee in the tiny charthouse immediately abaft the wheelhouse on the port side. The Doctor arrived and pronounced him dead.' **Lieutenant G J A Lumsden. RN.** [5]

Meanwhile the *Vimy* had also been loading its precious human cargo. During the operation her Captain, thirty-five year-old Lieutenant Commander Colin Donald, along with a Sub Lieutenant and Don Harris, had remained at key communications stations on the open bridge. The *Vimy* had taken about 700 people on board when she came under fire from the shore.

'Automatic rifle fire distinct from the shell-fire had been heard from the

bridge before I noticed our Captain train his binoculars on a hotel diagonally opposite but quite close to our ship. I heard another burst of firing from the snipers located in the hotel and then saw our Captain struck down. He fell onto his back and as I leaped to his aid I saw that a bullet had inflicted a frightful wound to his forehead, nose and eyes. He was choking in his own blood so I moved him onto his side, and it was then that I received his final order. It was, "get the First Lieutenant onto the bridge urgently". As I rose to my feet more shots from the hotel swept the bridge and the Sub-Lieutenant fell directly in front of me. I glanced down at him and saw four bullet holes in line across his chest. He must have been dead before he hit the deck. On the upper deck I located the First Lieutenant and appraised him briefly of what had occurred. He immediately assumed command and ordered all securing lines cast off and full speed astern. He consulted me on the approximate location of the snipers in the nearby hotel and after I had given my opinion he ordered "A" gun's crew up forward to bear on the target and fire a four inch shell at point blank range, no more than one hundred yards; the result was devastating indeed. Still at full speed astern we reached the outer limits of the harbour and then had to contend with German bombers. Our new temporary Captain performed a magnificent feat of seamanship as he manoeuvred his top heavy destroyer away from each attack. The planes broke away from us to attack the four French destroyers still at their task of bombarding the port. The first attack brought immediate results: the leading ship [L'Orage] suffered a direct hit and disappeared in a gigantic mushroom of flame and smoke. And so on to Dover to unload our human cargo, refuel, await a replacement Captain and try so very hard to get some precious sleep. Thus ended an episode which, the following day the London "Daily Mirror" reported under the banner headline, "THE HELL THAT WAS BOULOGNE". **Don Harris.**[6]

The inner harbour had now become a seething cauldron of battle. To the screeching of the diving Stukas and the scream of falling bombs was added the roar of naval guns and the staccato rattle of small arms fire. Huge geysers of mud and water erupted from the harbour basin as bombs hit the water around the ships. Shell splinters and lethal chips of granite from the harbour walls flew through the air.

On board the *Keith* the few minutes after Captain Simson's death were filled with chaos and confusion. Being above the level of the quay the bridge structure was exposed to bomb splinters and to the dismay of the crew on the bridge it now came under a murderous fire from small-arms and mortars originating from weapons in houses overlooking the berth from their port side. Bullets and fragments from mortar shells were freely piercing the steel sides of the wheelhouse and inevitably hitting frightened men and women packed inside and struggling to get down to the mess decks below. At the wheel, the Coxswain was spun around by a bullet hitting his steel helmet and the Torpedo Officer was hit in the arm as he crouched beside David Verney, a fellow officer, in the Captain's sea cabin. Verney fashioned a tourniquet using his handkerchief, a pencil, a rubber and a shoelace to try and stop the bleeding. All the soldiers who had scrambled onto the Flag Deck were killed. The First Lieutenant, himself wounded in the leg, now took command of the *Keith* and, following Admiralty guidelines, shouted at everybody to get down from his position at the starboard door of the wheelhouse. It was a bitter experience for men of the Senior Service to lie down on the deck under fire for minutes which seemed like hours. Lieutenant Lumsden found it an, 'undignified, unsuitable, indeed unacceptable position for a professional officer', and so he got to his feet remarking to the First Lieutenant that he had, '...had enough of it.' The *Vimy* had already cast off and the *Keith* was next to leave.

> *'The First Lieutenant, now our Captain, asked me if I could take the ship out. I had never commanded a ship going astern and certainly not down a narrow and curving channel peering through a small scuttle with bullets hitting people between me and the men who would carry out my orders!...I found myself replying "Of course I can Number One!" No communication was possible to the men on the upper deck to slip our wires, so after ringing on main engines I shouted engine orders to the Signal Officer and chief Yeoman of Signals, who were manning the telegraphs, to make the ship surge ahead and astern and so part the wires.'* Lieutenant G J A Lumsden. RN.[7]

Lumsden rushed up to the bridge more than once to improve his view astern but each time came clattering down again as bullets whistled about his ears. Keeping close to the stone pier on his port side the *Keith* rounded the bend in the channel and Lumsden increased her speed to fourteen knots.

> *'As we shot out of the harbour we passed the* Whitshed, *normally our flotilla second in command, going into Boulogne. We shouted to him that Captain Simson had been killed and warned him of the accurate small arms fire from the northern side of the harbour. Outside the harbour we manned the bridge and sorted out our load of disorderly refugees. Captain Simson and some dozen others were buried quietly at sea as we scanned the skies for enemy aircraft.'* Lieutenant G J A Lumsden. RN.[8]

Lumsden's fellow officer, David Verney later wrote,

> *'Our navigator, Lieutenant Lumsden, conned the ship from the chart house, breaking our berthing wires, and took the ship out stern first; it was just like a Wild West shootout!'*

Lumsden, although recommended for a medal, did not receive one as the *Keith* returned to Dover with 'less than a complete load of passengers'. Instead his fellow officers in the Wardroom presented him with the medal of the Chevalier of the Order of Oranje Nassau, which Queen Wilhelmina of the Netherlands had issued to the *Keith* for her assistance in evacuating the Dutch Royal family from Holland earlier that month.

HMS *Whitshed* then steamed into Boulogne harbour for the second time that day. Accompanied by HMS *Vimiera*, and berthing under the aegis of nine RAF fighters, both ships engaged German units and guns on the high ground to the north in and around Fort de la Creche. The two ships began loading mixed detachments of AMPC and strays from the BEF as fast as they could and Brigadier Fox-Pitt at last managed to get the evacuation message out to his battalion commanders in the field by dispatch rider. There were problems, however, in passing it down the chain of command. Lieutenant Colonel Stanier in particular found it difficult to get in touch with his company commanders and had to resort to delivering messages himself.

'As expected, Brigadier Fox-Pitt quite rightly decided to withdraw us and we took up a position half way through the town. Then we were told to withdraw to the quayside. Well the only way I could get them to withdraw was to go myself or send somebody else. So I sent somebody to the other three companies – but No. 3 Company who'd had the brunt of it in the morning, had got so far...I knew where they were, in a white house just near

Closing in. German troops working their way through factory buildings.

the crossroads in the middle of the town. I said "I know where they are...I know the street. I can find it, I'll go there." I went there and of course they were being shot at. So was I. I went to the door and it was locked and I banged on the door and did everything possible...I couldn't get anybody to open it. Eventually I couldn't stay there any longer. I mean there were too many bullets flying about, so I jumped into my car and my gallant driver drove me back down the street.' Lieutenant Colonel Sir Alexander Stanier Bt., MC. CO 2 Welsh Guards.⁹

Stanier later learned that one of the men had gone to Major Windsor-Lewis and told him that someone was banging on the door. Windsor-Lewis had decided to look out of the window before opening the door and removed the barricades just in time to see Stanier's car disappearing down the street. Jim Windsor-Lewis knew it had been his CO but had no idea of the importance of his visit. Ignorant of the evacuation order the remnants of 3 Company fought on as the rest of the battalion prepared to move to the

Brigadier Fox-Pitt (centre) checking troops across the Pont Marguet bridge. To his right Lieutenant Colonel Stanier with Major Jones-Mortimer on the Brigadier's left. Note the destroyer firing its guns in the background. Courtesy RHQ Welsh Guards

quays. The men of 4 Company greeted the news of evacuation with unconcealed delight.

'We were all in quite good form, sharing out what we had, when an order to close for embarkation came. Whoopee! We streamed to Company HQ and I led off for the quay...Eventually we all rushed across the bridge onto the quay. Billy Fox-Pitt, our Brigade Commander said we were late!!! and told us to go into a vast shed.' Second Lieutenant Peter Hanbury. OC 12 Platoon, 4 Company, 2 Welsh Guards.[10]

'We were in the town area where we were getting sniped at and we broke into a flat for shelter. In the kitchen were two or three tins of biscuits, sealed. The officer forbade us to touch these in case they had been tampered with and resealed. When we came from there, Captain Heber-Percy marched us down to the docks. The Germans had shelled the place quite a bit so there was loads of rubbish lying about. Amidst all this there was an old lady on some steps, above all things, cleaning her windows!'[11] Guardsman F E Smith. 1 Company 2 Welsh Guards.

Lieutenant Colonel Stanier had driven back to the Pont Marguet to meet Brigadier Fox-Pitt on the bridge. The naval demolition parties had already laid explosive charges and Fox-Pitt was eager to get the Welsh Guards

across before the Germans closed in.

'I went back and met Billy Fox-Pitt on the bridge, which gives access to the quay and we checked everybody through except, of course, No.3 Company. He said "I can't wait any longer, I am going to blow the bridge", which we then did, rather unsuccessfully as it happened, but we did enough damage to prevent vehicles getting through.' **Lieutenant Colonel Sir Alexander Stanier Bt., MC. CO 2 Welsh Guards.**[12]

The Welsh made their way onto the quays where the situation was still frantic and solid with troops even though the *Whitshed* and *Vimiera* had begun loading. The German tanks had followed the Welshmen down through the town and were now accompanied by half-track vehicles moving up and down the streets.

'You could see the tanks. We were in one cellar, and one passed us and we were worried stiff in case some bloody fool'd fire at him. We got to the harbour and we were in a wine cellar. All those houses had wine cellars loaded with all sorts of spirits and wine. 'Jerry' came down the street in this tank, quite happily with his head out the top and we daren't do anything – daren't say anything because if he knew we were in that cellar – one round and he'd have killed the lot of us, there were about five of us. The minute that tank went out of sight we were up and away and then we got on the harbour where all the trees were and then a plane started shooting at us. That was easy because you could step to one side behind a big tree and then when the plane came back you could step the other side. There were times when I was frightened to death but sometimes I wasn't worried I don't know

'Jerry came down the street in this tank, quite happily with his head out of the top.'

Above: A tank commander views the battlefield from the turret hatch of a Panzer Mk IV. One of the gunners operates a *Schmeisser* through a turret port. Note the Walther 9mm P-38 on the commander's belt.

Left: A Panzer major in the turret of a Mk IV.

Below: Driver's position in a Panzer Mk IV.

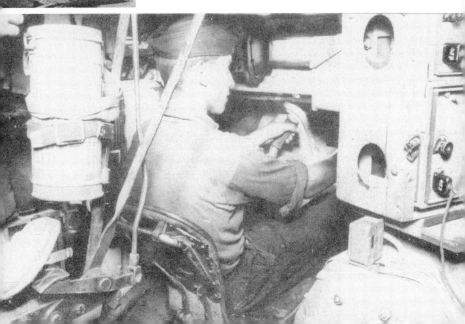

why. It was just a question of fighting right back to the beach.' Guardsman
Doug Davies. 8 Platoon, 3 Company, 2 Welsh Guards.[13]

It was now getting on for 8.00 pm. Fox-Pitt was told that evacuation would take place 'forthwith' and that a second flight of destroyers would come in to take off the Guards as soon as *Whitshed* and *Vimiera* had finished loading. There were very few Guardsmen on board. Amongst those who did embark were the survivors of the Brigade anti-tank platoon which the *Whitshed* had landed the previous day. A burly Irish guardsman climbed onto the *Whitshed's* bridge and placed a bottle of champagne onto the chart table. 'Thanks for the double ride', he said and disappeared. Lieutenant Colonel Haydon was later presented with a medallion bearing the *Whitshed's* crest – a demi-lion rampant holding a shamrock – by Commander E R Conder, her Captain, as a memento of her association with the Irish Guards.

The two destroyers cast off, each one taking about a thousand on board. Sergeant Arthur Evans was not on board the *Whitshed* as she sailed away carrying his comrades of the anti-tank platoon. At first light that morning he had resumed his painful withdrawal into town assisted by a guardsman at either side, after being wounded during the fighting on the outskirts of Outreau the previous evening.

> *'The next thing I can remember is lying on a stretcher on the dockside trying to protect myself from a couple of Stukas which were bombing the docks and harbour. An officer appeared and asked me if I wished to return to the UK on a ship which was about to leave. Fate stepped in – the fool! I declined his offer, saying I wished to stay in Boulogne with my battalion. An ambulance took me and others to a hospital up the hill near the old town. At the entrance the ambulance stopped and a medical orderly demanded my rifle and any ammunition I was carrying. To my astonishment, he threw the rifle onto a heap of others just inside the gate.'* Sergeant Arthur Evans, 2 i/c Anti-Tank Platoon, 2 Irish Guards. Attached 20 Guards Brigade.[14]

Wounded Guardsman Charles Thompson was, however, one of the lucky few.

> *'I was fortunate when a destroyer which had been standing off shore firing at the German tanks on the hill above, made a quick dash to pick us up and I was lucky to get on board. With guns blazing it headed back to the open sea. A Naval Medical Officer put me in his cabin and told me not to move. It was a relief to see the port of Dover again but I missed the White Cliffs because by now it was getting quite dark and obviously they had not the same meaning as when I had left a few days ago.'*
Guardsman Charles Thompson. 12 Platoon, 4 Company, 2 Welsh Guards.[15]

Thompson was sent to a hospital in Friern Barnet, London and his wounds were severe enough for him to be medically 'downgraded'. Two years later, at his own request, he was upgraded to 'A1' and in 1943 he joined 3 Welsh

Guards in North Africa.

Having got most of his battalion across the bridge Lieutenant Colonel Stanier opened his HQ in an empty railway carriage and set about chivvying his men along the quay to await the arrival of the promised destroyers with shouts of, 'Welsh Guards to the front, up to the top end Welsh Guards'. As soon as the *Whitshed* and the *Vimiera* were clear of the harbour HMS *White Swan* and HMS *Venomous* steamed in to take their places. They were followed swiftly by HMS *Venetia* and all three ships now began firing on German artillery positions to the north and on tanks and half-tracks in the streets around the harbour at a range of a few hundred yards. The *Venetia* was a few yards from the entrance to the harbour when a sheet of flame appeared to erupt from the hills near Fort de la Creche. The Germans had managed to get one of the French coastal guns working. All day since their capture of the Fort, a German artillery team had tried in vain to repair the guns which the French had failed to 'spike' irretrievably, then up stepped *Hauptfeldwebel* John, a veteran infantry gun man, then in command of an Engineer Platoon of 2 Motorcycle Battalion.

'Again and again he tries, adjusts the levers, turns the wheels and cogs – till suddenly it works! What the artillerymen tried to do in vain the motorcycle Hauptfeldwebel succeeds in. The first shot "thunders".'
Oberleutnant Durkes OC. 3 Company, 2 Motorcycle Rifle Battalion, 2 Panzer Division.[16]

'A motorcyclist company and an engineer storm troop have captured Fort de la Creche. A man is ordered to the telescope which allows him to see the English coast. The man...reports warships approaching. They are English destroyers. Unfortunately the crew of the fort and our own artillery had disabled the guns. Now one of the sergeants of the motorcycle company sets about a gun, and, while shell after shell hits the fort...the sergeant and some clever boys succeed in putting one of the guns in order. He does it calmly, smoking his pipe. He is sweating, black with dirt and oil, sometimes

One of the guns at Fort de la Creche is repaired and is brought into action against the British destroyers off Boulogne. Courtesy Herr Franz Steinzer

has to seek cover, but after half an hour he is able to fire the first shot, after a short time the next...The third shot hits one of the destroyers...the fourth to a hair hits the same destroyer. After the fifth shot the destroyer is set on fire and capsizes.' **Hubert Borchert.**[17]

The *Venetia* was struck amidships and the flames from the fire which broke out, were fanned towards her stern. Although she did not capsize as German accounts suggested she did develop a list. If she had been sunk in the narrowest part of the channel the whole evacuation enterprise would have been doomed to failure.

Meanwhile the *Wild Swan* and the *Venomous* had begun to embark the last of the wounded and the first parties of Guards. Requests from the commanders of the German rifle battalions, to allow their weary men to rest, were turned down as their superiors became aware that a complete evacuation was probably under way and that the capture of 20 Brigade was a possibility. For the next forty-five minutes the German guns, tanks and planes turned their attentions to the quay whilst the destroyers' guns replied in kind. One of the weary German soldiers roused from their rest to take part in the battle was *Oberfeldwebel* Langhammer.

Langhammer commanded a Panzer IV of the 4th (Heavy) Company of 3 Panzer Regiment. His crew had had a successful day. All the coastal fortifications to the south had been taken as the tanks of his company had advanced upon Boulogne and the captured French Marines had been escorted to the rear. He and his crew had been preparing supper and looking forward to their rest as they had watched the columns of smoke rising over Boulogne turned red by the rays of the setting sun. Langhammer's driver, Oskar Denscheilmann, had just opened a bottle of champagne on the tank's turret when the crew had heard the garbled voice of their company commander, *Oberleutnant* von Jaworski, carry over from a group of houses.

'What had I heard? Destroyer, harbour? Entering slowly? Panzer? – What's the matter? – And now I understand every word: "Down to the harbour immediately, we will spoil the destroyer's entrance." As quick as lightning we jump in our seats, already the engine growls and...our "Heinz" rushes with full speed following the commander. My men do not speak a word. They know what is lying ahead. I look at their faces. Fredi [Ivantschitz], *the loader, a Vienna boy, Leo* [Palmreuther], *the gunner; sitting ahead at the steering levers, the driver, one of the silent heroes of the Panzertruppe, his face dirty with dust and oil; "Sichel"* [Sichelstiel], *the wireless-operator, smiling as ever. Their eyes beam with resoluteness and a strong will to win. I give the first orders...The first marks are bridge, conning tower and gun "turrets" of the foredeck; the second mark is the engine room...Woe betide you destroyer, soon you will be acquainted with German panzers. Soon we are on the spot...the view curves across the hill*

down to the harbour. Now I see the commander dismounting the "car" ahead and with both arms he points forcefully to the harbour...Our neighbouring "car" has already opened fire. Passing it we feel the force of the muzzle blast inside our "car". But keep cool. We will see this cheeky intruder in his full size. Funnel, mast tops are already seen; an "Englishman". Further ahead. Standing on the forward slope without any cover we stop...A fire order is superfluous. Range 450 metres. Thundering, the first shell leaves the barrel. Will it be a direct hit? The flight seems perpetual. Then, lightning, a blue-glaring flash hits the mast: direct hit on the conning tower. Shouts of joy ring through the interior of our cockpit. The loader is working feverishly: three, four shells leave the barrel. 150-200 English infantrymen are to be seen clearly on the foredeck seeking cover...Too late, those who are not swept off the deck by the crushing effect of our shells jump overboard gesticulating wildly. We are shooting "quick fire"..."Schwupp" – again a shell is put into the barrel and soon it penetrates the thick armour of the gun "turret". Its turning is stopped abruptly, iron and steel splinters are whirling through the air. Finished. Suddenly...the tank is shaken by trembling and vibration. Splinters hit the right side of the panzer. Are we fired on? A heavy blow impacts less than two metres ahead of the bow armour. It's a struggle for life. Again our steel monster is trembling I realise that we are being strafed by AA guns and by ships' guns. Now aim well gunner. The fore deck is already burning. Thick black smoke rises and obscures the view. "Change target! Engine rooms!" I want to cry to my gun crew – in vain, biting smoke fills the compartment. It bites the throat and eyes. Tears are running incessantly down my face.

Gun crew in action in the confines of a Panzer Mk IV.

'A magnificent sight' HMS *Venetia* leaving Boulogne harbour stern first and ablaze after being hit by shells from Fort de la Creche.
Courtesy RHQ Welsh Guards

Soon the next shells are flying through the air and vanish into the hull. A cruel spectacle. Yes, "Tommy", you will learn who leaves the ground as the victor. Inexorably our shells destroy the installations of the ships interior. Ten or twelve shells are the conclusion of this rare fight, a fight of only a few minutes. In a wild drive back followed by the shell and shrapnel salvos of some enemy destroyers lying further out to sea, we hurry to our next cover. Here we may open the hatches. Cool air invades. I shake hands with my crew comrades. Our hearts are full of joy: We have managed it. Two hours later our destroyer, completely burnt out, goes to the bottom of the sea forever. Leutnant **Langhammer.**[18]

Langhammer was mistaken in his assertion that his crew had sunk a British destroyer. It is unlikely that a Panzer IV could have sunk a destroyer with its 75mm gun although at a range of 300 metres it could certainly have caused casualties and substantial damage to exposed structures. The official German *Wehrmachtsbericht* of Monday 27 May 1940 referred to Langhammer's company commander, *Oberleutnant* von Jaworski, in a brief sentence.

'Off Boulogne, an Oberleutnant in a Panzer Regiment, von Jaworski, with his panzer, shelled by several enemy warships, set a destroyer on fire.'

Unfortunately the event in question is not dated exactly but it is interesting to note that the official German report does not claim that a British destroyer was sunk only that one was set on fire.

By now the *Venetia*, just inside the breakwaters, was badly crippled. With German tanks firing at her from the Quai Gambetta she was set at full speed astern and skilfully taken out of the harbour towards the open sea and Dover, exchanging fire with the guns in and around Fort de la Creche.

> *'There was a terrific explosion on one of the destroyers...I don't know whether it was shell-fire or bombs, but the destroyer was left on fire. However, owing to magnificent seamanship, they were able to get her out so that she wouldn't block the harbour, which is what we thought would happen. She went out stern first – blazing at the stern and with all guns firing – a magnificent sight!'* Lieutenant Colonel Sir Alexander Stanier Bt., MC. CO 2 Welsh Guards.[19]

Amid the raging battle the Irish Guards moved down towards the inner side of the Quai Chanzy in sections and platoons and sheltered on its lower levels. They were deafened by the sound of the ships' guns above them,

Oberfeldwebel Langhammer and four of his crew. The unverified claim of a destroyer sunk is marked on the turret of his PzKpfw IV. The ship is identified by the numbers '523' and the date is '23.5.40". Courtesy Herr Franz Steinzer

The evening of 23 May, 1940, and as HMS *Venomous* slips out towards the sea a series of photographs of German shells bursting on the Princess Hotel are taken. The hotel survived the attack and stands today. It is presently used as a wine bar.

A pre war photograph for comparison.

Bren gun fire behind them and direct hits from German shells on the granite quays above. With the decks of the ships just yards away the Irish resolve was put to the test but no-one moved until Lieutenant Colonel Haydon gave the embarkation order himself. The discipline and control of the Guards earned the respect of the naval officers as they moved towards the *Venomous* and the *Wild Swan*. First the wounded were lowered from the quay and then the rest of the battalion jumped on board. The tide was still out and it was a long way from the quay to the decks. A number of the Irish fell into the water but were fished out by the sailors. At around 9.30 pm the call went out to the Bren gun squads covering the embarkation to come in and they came aboard *Wild Swan* at the double. By 9.30 the bulk of the Irish were aboard and ready to go as the gunners of the *Wild Swan*, according to *The History of the Irish Guards*, scored a direct hit on a German tank and sent it 'spinning like a cartwheel.'

Some of the Welsh were also embarking but the operation was not going as smoothly as that of the Irish. The German Luftwaffe chose that moment to bomb the harbour. Lieutenant Colonel Stanier dived under a railway truck for cover along with the Padre and Captain J Duncan. The bombs exploded all around and when the dust settled Stanier and the padre got up; Captain Duncan did not. There was not a mark on him and

The port of Boulogne receiving a pounding.

Stanier later surmised that Captain Duncan had been killed by the sheer force of the blast.

Stanier and his staff got all the men he could muster up to the pier at the far end of the quay and ushered them on board the *Venomous*. He knew he was short of a good many men but two intelligence officers who forced their way down the quays failed to find the missing Welsh Guards. A little after 9.30 pm both ships cast off, each one carrying some 900 men. Once clear of the harbour all became quiet and it was only when the ships docked at Dover around midnight that Stanier realised how many had been left behind. Unfortunately it was not only his 3 Company under Major Windsor-Lewis which had been left behind; there were many others from 2 and 4 Companies who had not managed to get on board and a very large contingent of Lieutenant Colonel Deane's AMPC which had been somewhat left to withdraw as best it could from its posts in the northern suburbs, and consequently had not been able to get across the Pont Marguet before it had been blown.

2 and 4 Companies had made to go forward towards the *Venomous* from

one of the huge, black sheds near the Gare Maritime when they had become caught up in the heaving, pushing scrum and cut off from the rest. Amid the confusion, 'an officer' had approached Captain Jack Higgon and told him that 'the last destroyer had left'. After a short conference between Higgon and Captain Cas Jones-Mortimer, commanding 2 Company, it had been decided that their two companies would try and make a break for it, through the German ring and along the coast in the direction of Etaples. It was getting on towards midnight when the party set out. Peter Hanbury later recalled the episode in his diary.

> 'Jack and Cas decided to fight their way out to Etaples, as the bridges to the east had been blown. Order of march, No 2 Company, AMPC, 4 Company – machine-gunned – rallied in yard where I saw Eddie [Beddingfield]. I was the rear platoon, and No. 2 Company was caught in a street by machine-guns firing on fixed lines. Jack worked his way up and silenced one with his pistol through a window...I went...forward to get orders from Jack...As I reached him I became entangled in some wires on the pavement and the tracer kept hitting the kerb about three inches above my feet. Jack said to get into the nearest house under cover. This I did and went fast asleep. Eddie and Dickie [Twining], with over half the company, could not contact us and so went back to the quay; a boat came in...and took Eddie, Dickie and half the Company home.' Second Lieutenant Peter Hanbury OC 12 Platoon, 4 Company, 2 Welsh Guards.[20]

To this day some of the men involved who did not get home, believe dark deeds were afoot that night.

> 'What amazed me most of all was, we got as far as the boat and they were loading and I'd picked up a stretcher and was carrying one of the boys up the gang plank. I'd only have had to put my foot over the side of the boat and I'd have been home but a fellow came up to me and said, "let me take over 'Pritch'. I'm a married man with a family." I let him take the stretcher and I went back to the lads. The Germans came over and bombed us and they decided to take the boat out and come back. It turned out that there was a "Fifth Columnist" amongst us and this "Fifth Columnist" said get out and go to the next port a little bit lower down and he took us out into town. By this time it was getting dark, and they took us down this street and they were waiting for us. Like lambs to the slaughter. Luckily Number 4 Company were at the back but the first lot, Number 2, walked into it. What was left of us slept in an hotel; they pushed us in the coal cellar and said they'd wake us up in the morning to say that the boat was in. In the meantime I'd met up with my friend, a Swansea boy I'd joined up with, and we decided we'd get out on our own and over to the harbour at the crack of dawn.' Guardsman Syd Pritchard. 11 Platoon, 4 Company, 2 Welsh Guards.[21]

Back on the quay HMS *Windsor* had put into the harbour under cover of darkness at around 11.00 pm. With little interference from the Germans she

As darkness falls on 23 May shells continue to strike the quayside. Here an Allied truck receives a direct hit. Courtesy Sir Beville Stanier Bt

managed to load the naval demolition parties and a few stragglers when the men of 4 Company under Second Lieutenants Beddingfield and Twining appeared on the dockside after the aborted attempt to break out towards Etaples. Hardly daring to believe their luck they gratefully boarded the *Windsor*, now holding 600 men in all, and sailed for home. The last ship to approach the stricken port did so in the early hours of 24 May. The Germans had by now withdrawn for the night, their troops being desperately in need of rest and reorganisation. On the quays near the Gare Maritime Lieutenant Colonel Deane and 600 of his Pioneers were preparing for their final stand which they thought would come at daybreak. They felt they had been left behind. The message that the bridges were to be blown had come too late for them to cross to safety and they had fought a stubborn rearguard action all the way back to the Pont Marguet where they had finally managed to clamber across the partially demolished bridge to some form of cover. The AMPC had held out until dark when some of Deane's men had been persuaded to join Major Higgon's party in its attempted break-out. Now, as the ship approached at around 1.40 am in total darkness, Colonel Deane signalled her with his torch. In an eerie silence the *Vimiera*, for the second time, backed up to the mole and stayed at her berth for almost an hour while she embarked the last 600 men of 5 Group AMPC and 800 other stragglers who had been left behind. Grossly overloaded, she slipped her wires and vanished into the

138

darkness of the Channel without a shot being fired. She was the last British ship to leave Boulogne before it fell into German hands.

Sometime around midnight the exhausted Welsh and Irish Guards who had been evacuated reached Dover and after a hot meal they boarded trains for Fleet at around 4.30 am on 24 May *en route* for camp on Tweseldown racecourse. Just before they boarded the train the Welsh were overjoyed to see Second Lieutenant Twining and Second Lieutenant Beddingfield arrive with fewer than twenty men of 4 Company who had got away on HMS *Windsor*. It was impossible to provide an accurate breakdown of casualties at that early stage but Lieutenant Colonel Stanier calculated that of 944 other ranks who had embarked for Boulogne either with 2 Welsh Guards or attached to 20 Brigade, only 623 had come home, sixty-two of which were quickly evacuated to hospital. Only four men had been confirmed killed in action but of the other 317 there was no information. They could only be posted as 'missing'. Of his thirty-five officers, Stanier knew that Captain Duncan and Second Lieutenant Hexey Hughes had been killed but eleven more, including three of his company commanders were missing. It did not need a mathematician to work out that roughly a third of his battalion had been lost. Lieutenant Colonel Haydon had sailed for Boulogne with 699 men of

Lieutenant Colonel Sir Alexander Stanier Bt., MC.

all ranks and after the first roll call in England he found that his casualties amounted to 196 other ranks and five officers, two of which, Lieutenants Reynolds and Leveson, had been killed in action. As in Stanier's case, Haydon's losses were almost a third of his force.

Back across the Channel some of the men who made up those casualty statistics were in hospitals, manning barricades or huddled in small groups in the darkened cellars of houses. In the foreboding silence of the town after the earlier din of battle some of the Welsh Guards who had been left behind were pondering their fate. For the time being Syd Pritchard and about twenty other ranks along with Peter Hanbury and Major Cas Jones-Mortimer, made themselves as comfortable as possible in their cellar and waited to see what daylight would bring. Across the street Captains Jack Higgon and Henry Coombe-Tennant accompanied by Second Lieutenant Ion Garnett-Orme and thirty other ranks did the same. Guardsman Doug Davies, by now leaderless, was still sheltering in a cellar near the fish market. His CO Major Windsor-Lewis was still defending a road-block with his two forward sections somewhere in the town, oblivious to the fact that the battalion had been evacuated. Joseph Bryan was still alone somewhere up near St. Martin beyond the Haute Ville where General

Lanquetot and his French garrison had so far successfully resisted German pressure against the Citadel. General Lanquetot, Jim Windsor-Lewis, Syd Pritchard, Doug Davies and Joseph Bryan knew nothing of the dramatic events that had taken place at the harbour. As far as General Lanquetot and Windsor-Lewis were concerned the battle for Boulogne was still on and they were preparing for the next round. Little did Windsor-Lewis realise that for him and a small force of men, including Pritchard and Davies, the next round would be the last.

1. Lieutenant G J A Lumsden. RN. IWM Dept of Documents – 66/24/1.
2. Don Harris. IWM Dept. of Documents – 5/2/85.
3. IWM Dept. of Documents – 93/28/4.
4. *Oberleutnant* Dietz. *Abbeville und Boulogne unter den Schlagen einer Panzerdivision in Guderian Generaloberst H* (Ed) *Mit den Panzern in Ost und West.* Vol. 1.
5. Lieutenant G J A Lumsden. RN. *op.cit.*
6. Don Harris *op.cit.*
7. Lieutenant G J A Lumsden. RN. *op.cit.*
8. *ibid.*
9. Lieutenant Colonel Sir Alexander Stanier Bt., MC. CO 2 Welsh Guards. *Gort's Army – The British Expeditionary Force of 1939-1940.* IWM Sound Archive – 7175/7.
10. Second Lieutenant Peter Hanbury. OC 12 Platoon, 4 Company, 2 Welsh Guards. *A Not Very Military Experience.*
11. Guardsman F E Smith. 1 Company 2 Welsh Guards. Letter to author.
12. Lieutenant Colonel Sir Alexander Stanier Bt., MC. CO 2 Welsh Guards. *Sammy's Wars.*
13. Guardsman Doug Davies. 8 Platoon, 3 Company, 2 Welsh Guards. Author's tape transcript.
14. Sergeant Arthur Evans, 2 i/c Anti-Tank Platoon, 2 Irish Guards. Attached 20 Guards Brigade. *Sojourn in Silesia.*
15. Guardsman Charles Thompson.12 Platoon, 4 Company, 2 Welsh Guards. Account sent to author.
16. *Oberleutnant* Durkes OC 3 Company, 2 Motorcycle Rifle Battalion, 2 *Panzer* Division in Strauss F J. *Friedens-und Kriegserlebnisse einer Generation. Ein Kapitel Weltgeschichte aus der Sicht der Panzerjager-Abteilung 38(SF) in der ehemaligen 2 (Wiener) Panzerdivision.*
17. Hubert Borchert. *Panzerkampf im Westen.*
18. *Leutnant* Langhammer, 'Deutsche Panzer gegen englische Zerstorer' in Guderian H, (Ed) *Mit den Panzern in Ost und West, Vol 1.* Berlin 1942.
19. Lieutenant Colonel Sir Alexander Stanier Bt., MC. CO 2 Welsh Guards. *Lecture Notes in the possession of Sir Beville Stanier.*
20. Second Lieutenant Peter Hanbury *op.cit*
21. Guardsman Syd Pritchard. 11 Platoon, 4 Company, 2 Welsh Guards. Author's tape transcript.

CHAPTER NINE

MY LITTLE FORCE FOUGHT
MOST SPLENDIDLY

It was after 'stand to' at dawn on the morning of 24 May when Major Windsor-Lewis sent a messenger to search for the rest of his battalion. The messenger was the fourth that Windsor-Lewis had sent out since the time he had first withdrawn into Boulogne from his positions near the Mont Lambert crossroads. The first three messengers had not returned, Windsor-Lewis assuming they had been retained at Battalion HQ due to the heavy firing in the town. Now, the small band of 3 Company under their charismatic CO – the only officer in the company left to command a body of men after the fighting on the morning of 23 May – anxiously awaited news of their battalion.

They had spent an uncomfortable night at their road blocks. Shortly after dusk the previous evening, at roughly the same time the bulk of 2 Welsh Guards had sailed for home, two German panzers with infantry creeping behind had approached Windsor-Lewis's position and had been driven off. Shortly afterwards his men had been machine-gunned from

A road block on a street behind the Boulevard Gambetta.
Courtesy RHQ Irish Guards

houses opposite and two houses on his left flank had burst into flames. It was not until after midnight that the firing had died down and his exhausted men had been able to get some fitful rest until time came for them to 'stand to' just before dawn.

Unlike the first three messengers, the fourth returned with the shocking news that the battalion 'had gone.' Windsor-Lewis decided to move to the quayside as quickly as possible with the men he had left. In spite of the heavy presence of German tanks and half-tracks in and around the harbour

The German caption for this photograph, taken at a British road block, reads 'At the harbour of Boulogne the enemy is still resisting'. With the fighting still going on a German soldier peers warily around the corner. Bundesarchiv Koblenz

area the previous evening, the party were not troubled during their short march to the quay which required them to pick their way over the partially demolished bridge towards the area of the Gare Maritime where a scene of chaos greeted them.

'On arrival at quayside with the remnant of my company I found the utmost confusion in progress. There were stragglers from No. 2 and 4 Companies, 2WG., some Irish Guards, about 150 refugees, 120 French soldiers with 2 officers, 200 of the AMP's, 120 men of RE and others. I collected this force in the sheds by the station while I, with a Major EGM Burt of the RE...went off to find the minesweeper which had just come into the harbour and ask if it would evacuate us to England.' Major J C Windsor-Lewis, OC 3 Company, 2 Welsh Guards.

Windsor-Lewis crossed the damaged bridge to speak to the senior French officer aboard the minesweeper who declined to evacuate the quay but said that when he put to sea once more he would signal to any boat or warship he saw to go to their rescue. A staff officer on the quay had already told Windsor-Lewis that whilst the brigade had been evacuated, boats were supposed to be returning for the men left behind. Windsor-Lewis then tried to re-cross the bridge and came under heavy machine gun fire from houses close to the harbour. Dodging behind abandoned cars and the litter of equipment he managed to get back to his men unscathed.

Syd Pritchard and his pal, Guardsman Bert Jeffers, who had taken part in the aborted attempt to break out of Boulogne the night before, had also decided to make their way to the harbour early that morning.

'Friday morning we made our way to the harbour across the big bridge and we caught up with Windsor-Lewis. We fought Friday morning until 2 o'clock on Saturday 25 May, non-stop. We were in a coal cellar. "Jeff" and I used our initiative and before crack of dawn we got up quietly and we covered each other dodging between the vehicles that were left on the front. He covered me; I covered him so many yards. How we got through was a miracle. I don't where "Jerry" was, he must have been "standing down" because we had plenty of cover. "Jerry" was in the town then. How we did it I don't know to this day because it meant coming along the harbour dodging between cars and what have you that the French had put there, we

Elements of a German infantry division passing through a French town in May 1940.

got from that cellar along the harbour wall, across the big bridge, which was a miracle, and then we met Major Lewis the other side. We were under Major Lewis's guidance after that. Guardsman Syd Pritchard. 11 Platoon, 4 Company, 2 Welsh Guards.[2]

Doug Davies had also decided that his best chance of escape lay in getting to the harbour. From his shelter behind the stinking dustbins of the fish market he also managed to get across the bridge and was overjoyed to find his company commander on the other side.

Major Windsor-Lewis now applied himself to the defence of the quays around the Gare Maritime. The cavernous sheds were packed with troops and refugees and Lieutenant Kenneth Roscoe of the RE was dispatched into the station itself to find out if it provided better cover and if it could be defended. On Roscoe's return Windsor-Lewis, who had by now assumed command of the composite Allied force, moved all the refugees back into the shelters on the lower levels of the Gare Maritime itself. Soon afterwards the Germans, now realising that not all the Allied troops had escaped, opened fire on the sheds with small arms and shells from tanks, wounding several men. Windsor-Lewis immediately began to withdraw the men into the station under cover of the trucks and carriages of two trains, one of which was an empty hospital train, standing motionless at the platforms on either side of the station. Amongst the first out were Syd Pritchard and Bert Jeffers.

'First of all we had to crawl under the wagons. He wanted two single men. I drew the short straw, I had to go first but that's the luck of the draw isn't it. He wanted us to go and come back and tell them if there was anybody left. In the meantime the Germans blew up the black shed; they set it on fire. "Jeff" and I had gone out we would have gone back, instead of that it was up in flames and they were coming to meet us, the boys and the evacuees; all the women and the children who were in there. They were all crouched in the corner when we'd found them.' Guardsman Syd Pritchard. 11 Platoon, 4 Company, 2 Welsh Guards.[3]

The German fire had by now increased and they turned their attentions to the station itself.

'For about an hour they just fired bullets into the station. They fired and fired and fired before that black shed went up. That's where a lot got wounded. Major Lewis had a big five-foot wall of sandbags and we went there after. Syd and I met on the station.' Guardsman Doug Davies. 8 Platoon, 3 Company, 2 Welsh Guards.[4]

The sandbags were a godsend for Windsor-Lewis. They had been found in the station itself and he quickly set the many unarmed AMPC men to work building a breastwork in front of the station itself and on the left flank overlooking the town and the Customs House, whilst the Welsh Guards and French troops took up positions under cover and behind the trains.

Doug Davies and Syd Pritchard were two of those ordered to take up fire positions behind one of the two trains, which were now coming under heavy fire from German tanks and machine-guns positioned just 400 metres away across the water of the Bassin a Flot , the present day Bassin Napoléon.

'Imagine a big train station that's what it was and this train of ours was nearer to the water than the others. There was no platform on the water side. We were three in a train and the train had sliding doors and we had just a few sand bags and we were firing at these tanks. They were firing across the water at our train from the tanks. An officer was standing outside his tank and he couldn't care less what we were throwing at him. Then they must have fired a million bullets, just kept firing at the station. Underneath were the Pioneer Corps...' **Guardsman Doug Davies. 8 Platoon, 3 Company, 2 Welsh Guards.**

'At the black bridge the Red Cross carriages were all lined up beyond and there was a landing stage for the boats. On top it was like Euston all under cover. We had sandbags but there weren't many. We sand bagged up the different doorways and used what we had for cover, any opening, the door between two carriages. Another good place was underneath between the railway track and the wheel. The wheel itself gave you a good view out. They had you measured all along. We saw a "Jerry" tank sitting right opposite on the other side of the harbour. You couldn't fire freely because you didn't have the ammunition. When ours had gone – the fifty bandolier – you were picking it up that had been left behind. A lad called Pugh was killed at the station. He's on his own in Boulogne [cemetery]. I'm convinced that they've got the dates wrong. He was killed on the 24th, on the Friday, underneath an ambulance coach between two bogey wheels. I'd been there before him – in that position.' **Guardsman Syd Pritchard. 11 Platoon, 4 Company, 2 Welsh Guards.**

By midday the Allied force had established as good a defensive position as it could under such trying circumstances. All those holding the position were already exhausted and there was

146

very little food and water to go round. For the rest of the day the Germans poured fire into the station and the trains as they tried to secure the harbour.

After a days rest, *Leutnant* Künzel and the rest of his motorcycle platoon had by now moved up into the suburbs of Boulogne itself after their fight against Sergeant Arthur Evans's anti-tank gun on the evening of 22 May.

'Together with panzers – behind each of them a MG squad – we advance through the town...Cautiously we secure to all sides; the advance is slow for all cellars are to be searched...After having mopped up some streets we approach the channel which divides Boulogne in two...In the channel are three patrol trawlers and several small merchantmen. On the other side there is, to the right, a railway station with several trains side by side, in the foreground a hospital train. The two panzers placed under the command of my platoon are brought up to the right and to the left at the corners of the houses whereas we mount our MG in the first floor of the half destroyed houses. In the moment when I was assigning covering parties for the

The Belgian hospital train at the Gare Maritime with red crosses marked on the carriage roofs. The Germans were furious when they were fired upon from the direction of these carriages.
Bundesarchiv Koblenz

panzers, vivid machine-gun fire starts from the hospital train mixed with the bangs of English anti-tank rifles. With a jump we take cover behind the tanks and the bullets hit the walls of the houses opposite. Now we start fireworks which totally stuns them over there. We reply to the enemy's contravention of international law with all the weapons we have. Through the binoculars I clearly observe the doors of the hospital train to be protected with sand bags and that behind them are mounted MG's or anti-tank rifles. Mortars forward! The distance is taken and...the light mortar is positioned behind a panzer on the cobble stone pavement and aimed 'over a thick thumb'. The first grenade falls into the water, the second, third and fourth fall just behind the train, the fifth penetrates...above the anti-tank rifle and the five other grenades hit the train on different spots...For some minutes there is no more shooting. We observe a tricolor to be waved above a loop-hole. Will they surrender? I stand up beside a panzer and shout across, "Soldats francais, montrez le drapeau blanc et nous ne tirerons plus". Then, a Frenchman appears before the train and lies down. I repeat my demand and order him to get up. He does so and disappears. Shortly afterwards there is shooting again from over there. Damned bastards! We reply with a hurricane of fire. An anti-tank gun is drawn forward and destroys an anti-tank rifle. After the mortar is aimed at the patrol trawler lying before the train it is finally quiet. In the meantime No. 2 and No. 3 platoon have mopped up the whole block and have about eighty Englishmen come out of the cellars.' Oberleutnant **Künzel.**[7]

It was not the first time, nor would it be the last that front line soldiers would accuse those on the other side of an abuse of the Red Cross symbol but in many cases such accusations were probably based on errors of observation. The Allied troops were defending sections of the hospital train, albeit a hospital train from which all the wounded had been removed. The carriages which bore the Red Cross, however, were backed up towards the Pont Marguet and Syd Pritchard remains convinced that no Allied troops fired from them. Pritchard was by turns, in or under some of the unmarked carriages nearest the Gare Maritime and as far as he was concerned he was fighting for his life.

At about 6.00 pm a small party of German infantry attempted to attack Windsor-Lewis's right flank by crossing the Bassin a Flot in a small boat, but were driven back by rifle, anti-tank rifle and Bren gun fire. It was at this time too that the first German artillery shells began to land on the narrow neck of land leading to the Gare Maritime.

Sometime around 10.00 pm the German fire died away and Windsor-Lewis was able to take some of the men like Pritchard and Davies out of the front line for a rest in relays. They had held the Germans at bay for a whole day. The question was, how long they could hold on?

The Germans had now occupied the whole town except for the Haute

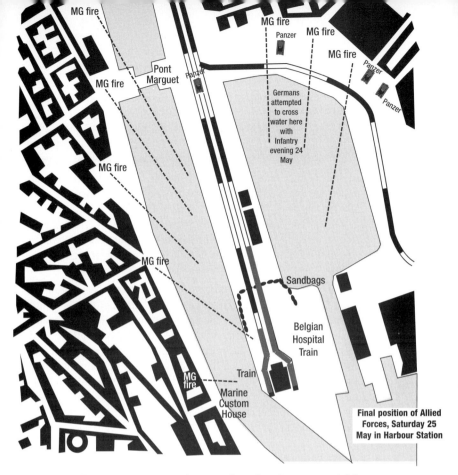

MG fire

MG fire

Panzer

MG fire

MG fire

Panzer

Pont
Marguet

Panzer

MG fire

Panzer

Germans
attempted
to cross
water here
with
Infantry
evening 24
May

MG fire

MG fire

MG fire

Sandbags

Belgian
Hospital
Train

Train

MG
fire

Marine
Custom
House

**Final position of Allied
Forces, Saturday 25
May in Harbour Station**

Ville and the Gare Maritime and it was clear that they were winkling out parties of British soldiers who had not managed to get away on board the destroyers. Second Lieutenant Peter Hanbury and his fifty or so comrades were, however, not amongst the prisoners. Although Syd Pritchard and Bert Jeffers had taken matters into their own hands at first light to try and get to the port and Major Jones-Mortimer had disappeared along with Second Lieutenant Ion Garnett Orme to try and get in touch with the French, Hanbury had stayed put. He and the remaining officers spent the whole of Friday 24 May venturing cautiously from their hiding places to search for food from neighbouring houses. Intermittent shelling and machine gun fire went on all day and although panzers rattled ominously past the end of their street none of them ventured down it. The officers had no maps and everyone was by now thoroughly exhausted. The odds were stacked against them.

*'We hoped if we could improve the men's morale we might make a break
or that the Marines would come...I was now so tired my brain became*

numb. Day merged into night, as I had not slept properly for three nights. Either Peter [Black] or I were always going round sentries, while the other one was out scavenging for food.' Second Lieutenant Peter Hanbury. OC 12 Platoon, 4 Company, 2 Welsh Guards.[8]

Corporal Joseph Bryan had trudged down the hill into town from St. Martin alone that morning. Although the Germans were by now on all sides he had walked as far as the high stone ramparts of the Haute Ville and had seen neither hide nor hair of them. He little knew that he was about to become involved in the French defence of the Old Town.

'On the way down I passed an old castle and as I was passing there, there was another "Tommy" from the Service Corps I think. A French officer came to the edge of the wall, and waved for us to go in and as we went in he pointed to a gun and said "you can take turns manning it".' Corporal Joseph Bryan. 2 Welsh Guards attached 20 Guards Brigade Anti-Tank Company.[9]

Isolated in his HQ in the rue d'Hautmont behind the protective walls of the Haute Ville, the French General Pierre Lanquetot learned of the departure of 20 Guards Brigade with dismay. He had had precious little contact with Brigadier Fox-Pitt and the commanding officers of the two battalions of Guards since their arrival on the morning of 22 May. Lanquetot's first HQ in the chateau de la Caucherie was but a stone's throw north of the initial positions of 3 Company of the Welsh Guards at the Mont Lambert cross-roads and even then he had had no contact with Lieutenant Colonel Stanier. It appeared, to French eyes at least, that the British had arrived in Boulogne with one aim in mind: to act unilaterally in the defence of the port.

Lanquetot had not been informed of the decision to land 20 Brigade in Boulogne and now, towards dawn on 24 May, he found that the British had departed during the night and once again he had been left in the dark. Worse still, a substantial part of the force he had reckoned on using to defend the town were by now safe on the other side of the English Channel. Even if the British had told him of their intentions it would have made little difference to Lanquetot. After the departure of the British he received an order from the French Admiral Abrial that he was to fight on come what may.

Lanquetot had moved his HQ to the Haute Ville on the evening of 22 May when he learned that the Germans had pushed a patrol between his HQ and the Welsh Guards in St. Martin. He had ordered all documents to be burned and had driven to the Citadel where he had abandoned his car in front of the Cathedral of Notre Dame. On his arrival Lanquetot had found a mixed garrison of French soldiers, sailors and marines defending the four main gates and lining the ancient ramparts which enclosed the Old Town. *Commandant* Berriat had organised the defence of the Château in the north-east corner whilst the ramparts were being held by infantry under

A scene of devastation outside the walls of the Haute Ville opposite the Porte Neuve. Note the damage to the wall to the right of the gate and the woman sitting on the bench between the disabled cars in the foreground.

Bundesarchiv Koblenz

Lieutenant Colonel Santini and the remnants of 13 *Regiment Regionale* under Colonel Wimet who had fought their way up to the Haute Ville the day before. They had been amongst the lucky few who had managed to escape to the relative safety of the Old Town. Of the rest of the French soldiers and marines who, during the night of 22/23 May, had been ordered to hold key points in four sectors of the town by General Caille, commanding the infantry of Lanquetot's 21 Division, many had been killed or captured and the rest were still holding on stubbornly.

At the semaphore of the Tour d'Odre on the cliff tops overlooking the

Jean-François L'Her

Boulevard Ste. Beuve, and the Casino, the 200 strong force under *Commandant* Henri Nomy had been captured at around 5.00 pm on 23 May after savage hand to hand fighting. *Premier Maitre* Jean Francois L'Her had been killed after shooting dead a German soldier who had been trying to cut down the French Tricolor. At the Pont de la Lampe a small force under *Capitaine* Sudre had fired their one and only 75mm field gun at the Germans until they too had been overwhelmed and killed. A little further along the bank of the Liane another party under *Commandant* Denneze were still hanging on. At the casino near the foot of the cliffs at the southern end of the Boulevard Ste. Beuve, another single 75mm gun and a force of 200 marines under the command of *Lieutenant de Vaisseau* de Saint-Remy had managed to hold out all day on 23 May but they were now desperately short of ammunition and almost surrounded. Beyond the walls of the Haute Ville in the streets to the south of the Porte Gayole, an area which had not as yet come under heavy attack, Lieutenant Colonel Franclieu and the men of his 417 Pioneers still held the Germans at bay from strong points in and around the rue Porte Gayole. Throughout the morning of 24 May the French braced themselves for the German assault which was launched in the afternoon.

'*13h. Like a tiger the Division leaps against the enemy desperately defending himself. In exemplary co-operation between panzers and infantry the eastern part of Boulogne is occupied. The Division commander himself [Veiel] is leading the combat, his officers assault at the head of their units...behind a ten to twelve metre high and uninterrupted wall of medieval origin the enemy has entrenched himself excellently. Artillery and Heavy Flak is thrown forward and is firing directly against the wall – in vain, the attack stops before the Cathedral. A half hour's burst of fire by the heavy mortar battalion with subsequent assault remains without results. Again and again the men assault. Up and down the struggle rages. Hours pass away.*' Oberleutnant **Dietz.**[10]

The severity of the assault forced the French defenders on the Route de Calais and the streets around the rue Porte Gayole to fall back to the ramparts. It was a bitter struggle. The small force under *Lieutenant de Vaisseau* de Saint-Remy at the Casino held out until around 2.00 pm until they too gained permission to fight their way back up the hill to the Haute Ville as did the rest of *Commandant* Denneze's party near the Pont de la Lampe. At 2.15 General Lanquetot ordered the symbolic burning of the 65 Infantry Regiment's flag in the presence of General Caille and *Commandant* Rosmorduc, the OC of the 48 Infantry Regiment.

By 6.45 pm the Germans had fought their way to the foot of the ramparts but such was the ferocity of the resistance that they made little headway against the ancient walls. At around 8.00 pm a fresh attack fell against the Chateau, the Porte de Calais (Porte Neuve) and the Porte des Dunes. Again the Germans were held. *Commandant* Berriat defending the Château refused the surrender demands of two emissaries sent from General Veiel.

As darkness fell the Germans were still hammering at the walls and the fire continued throughout the hours of darkness. During the night General Guderian himself visited the forward HQ of the left Combat Group and took a telephone call from General Veiel. After the call he replaced the receiver slowly and sat down heavily in his chair. 'Boulogne is to be captured today, gentlemen' he said. 'The troops are to be informed.'

Guderian discusses tactics with his officers.

Inside the Citadel, Lanquetot, still in touch with Admiral Abrial in Dunkirk, received permission to attempt a breakout at midnight but the hour passed and no attempt was made, however General Caille, Lanquetot's Chief of Staff, Colonel Barande and *Commandant* Rosmorduc with an advance guard of fifteen men managed to escape through the German ring.

During the small hours of 25 May Lanquetot realised that it would be impossible to maintain the struggle for much longer. The Germans had cut the water supply, there was little food and ammunition was running out. Although the men in the Château and the Porte Gayole were holding on, the situation at the Porte des Dunes was precarious. Towards dawn on 25 May the Germans launched their final assault and resorted to siege tactics reminiscent of centuries past. Bringing up two 88mm anti-aircraft guns the Germans fired them point blank at the ramparts at two specific points; the first opposite the Rue Flahaut and the other just to the north of the Porte de Calais. With *Oberst* von Vaerst, OC 2 Schützen Brigade, directing the fire of the 88mm flak guns personally the thick walls began to yield under the relentless bombardment and eventually the walls were reduced almost to ground level. By 5.30 am, using scaling ladders, storming parties had broken into the Haute Ville in two places.

> '*Flak rages against the Cathedral. A breach is made by direct shelling at close range. Soon the first storm troops assault with flame throwers and hand grenades by means of ladders crossing the wall. A fighting group at the north-east side is inside the Citadel. After a short time the enemy, defending desperately, is unable to stop the breach of the other fighting group.*' Oberleutnant Dietz.[11]

The battle raged on as the French fought for every stone of the Old Town. At 8.00 am two French prisoners carrying white flags approached the Porte de Calais with a German ultimatum for Lanquetot. 'If the Citadel does not surrender Boulogne will be burned.' Realising the futility of carrying on Lanquetot contacted Admiral Abrial in Dunkirk by telephone and was given permission to surrender but asked the Germans for time to convey the ceasefire message to the rest of the garrison.

It was at this time that Corporal Joseph Bryan's war came to an end. After being waved into the Haute Ville by a French officer the previous day he had found his way down a little alleyway which led to a small room: windowless on the wall facing the road but with boards covering the windows on the other side. He was in there with four Belgian soldiers when the Germans broke through.

> '*There was a real blast and a German soldier standing at the entrance had thrown some blast bombs in the alleyway and it blew the windows out that had been boarded up. I looked out onto a mass of soldiers all French with backpacks ready to go. It was like looking down from the stand onto a*

German storming parties succeed in breaking into the Haute Ville using scaling ladders. From a contemporary German sketch.

soccer field and the field was filled. I wondered later why a French officer had waved us in to man a gun when there were thousands of them there packed ready to go. That was the end of my tour of France. I was the only 'Tommy', plus the other one, that I could find or see anywhere. We were marched further north towards the border and that's where we came together with some prisoners from Calais and later on some from Dunkirk.'

Corporal Joseph Bryan. 2 Welsh Guards attached 20 Guards Brigade Anti-Tank Company.[12]

These were the French soldiers who had heard of the surrender but the garrison in the Château were still fighting. A party of German pioneers assaulted the Château even as the bulk of the French were laying down their arms, and *Commandant* Berriat's party fought on unaware of the ceasefire. Lanquetot was taken to see Guderian and Veiel and a message was sent to the 300 exhausted defenders of the Château urging them to cease fire. This they did and at 10.30 am the men marched out of the Porte de Calais towards the area known as the 'Dernier Sou' under the gaze of

Oberstleutnant Decker OC 2 Schützen Regiment who was fulsome in his praise of the heroic French resistance.

Isolated pockets of French troops, oblivious of the surrender, fired on the Germans, shooting two near the Tour Francoise and another near the Porte des Dunes. It was the middle of the afternoon when the machine gun of Lieutenant Duplantier of the 417 Pioneers, firing from a building on the Rue Port Gayole, was finally silenced.

By the time Duplantier had been killed the final curtain had also fallen on Major Windsor-Lewis's defence of the Gare Maritime.

The Germans had attacked just after 'stand to' on the morning of 25 May when the French infantry were holding the line and several men had been lost. Some time around 9.00 am Windsor-Lewis had scanned the high ground above the town through his

The heroic French resistance in the Haute Ville is finally crushed. German troops secure the Rue Port Neuve.

binoculars and had seen large bodies of troops on the move. He had hoped that these might be French troops coming to his rescue but it soon became clear that they were German forces moving in to consolidate the town.

Shortly afterwards the German artillery had opened up and another big

The Central Station completely destroyed. It stood near the site of the Foyer du Marin between the Ponts Marguet and Entente Cordiale. Bundesarchiv Koblenz

shed had been blown to pieces. The wounded were now being 'knocked about' considerably. Major Windsor-Lewis had then gone out in a desperate bid to find an escape route to his right but two German tanks had the right flank covered. At noon Guardsmen Syd Pritchard and Doug Davies plus another man were back in position near the train to the west of the station itself and at this point the Germans, now strongly reinforced, hit Windsor-Lewis's position with increased venom.

'We had a roll call at the end and Lewis said "get the guardsmen together and I'll tell them what's happening". He told chaps "so many up there, so many in the front" in the hot-spot right in the front line. Everybody was dirty and everybody did their stint. Lewis told us there was no hope – there was no way we were getting back. We were on this train, just the three of us firing. Windsor-Lewis was behind us with a load of sand bags, with no more than ten blokes and we did not know he had put the white flag up and we were firing. That's when they blew us out of the flippin' train because we were firing after the white flag had gone up. I always say that Syd and I were among the last three blokes in action at Boulogne; we had to be because they'd put the white flag up!' Guardsman Doug Davies. 8 Platoon, 3 Company, 2 Welsh Guards.[13]

'I was under the impression that it was put up against his wishes. I think the French interfered there and he shot it down. According to Major Windsor-Lewis the Germans issued an ultimatum. He called a few of us together. He said, "destroy everything you've got, every mortal thing". They'd sent over an ultimatum, "If you don't surrender by 2 o'clock we'll blow you out". The French had attempted to put the white flag up two or three times and he'd sent somebody out to tear it down...but you didn't give up hope until the very end.' Guardsman Syd Pritchard. 11 Platoon, 4 Company, 2 Welsh Guards.[14]

The end was not long in coming. Such was the ferocity of the German onslaught that Windsor-Lewis decided to move back into the station itself, '...protected only by glass overhead and by a train on the left flank.' It was a desperate situation and although his men saw Windsor-Lewis as a 'fearless' leader, he had others to think of besides himself and his Welsh Guards.

'There was little food and ammunition left and no more water, and after another hour of the greatest discomfort I decided my position was quite hopeless and that a massacre would ensue if I did not capitulate. Having an eye to the number of refugees under my care and the big percentage of unarmed men I decided to surrender.' Major J C Windsor-Lewis, OC 3 Company, 2 Welsh Guards.[15]

Doug Davies recalled the ferocity of the German attack on the train in the last few minutes before he was compelled to escape towards the station where he was finally taken prisoner along with Syd Pritchard.

'I remember the last few minutes more or less being blown out of that train hearing bullets coming in – da da da da da da da – and we went to Major Lewis behind the sandbags and we just waited for the Germans to come. We'd finished our fighting. I'd used my ammunition. I could have got some I've no doubt but there was no point. Major Lewis said we'd finished. We just waited for the Germans to come and take us out. They were coming over the bridge. You can't describe how you felt, terrible, terrible. They took your watches off, your rings off. There was no problem with their attitude at all. No brutality or anything like that, they just came as normal blokes. I had shrapnel wounds – lot of blood but no damage and they, the front line troops, made you take your jacket off and they bandaged it up. They did it with all of us.' Guardsman Doug Davies. 8 Platoon, 3 Company, 2 Welsh Guards.[16]

'I was downstairs, that's where I was when "Jerry" came in and I was giving water to a chap who was wounded and a German officer came up and spoke in perfect English.. He'd been wounded – shrapnel – big, tall fellow; a tank commander and he complimented Major Lewis on such a good fight. He said, "that's all you are?" He was surprised by the small number of people we had. It was double figures but it was only a handful. I was leaning down by this wounded boy on a stretcher giving sips of water and he spoke

to me, a proper gentleman – didn't search me – and said, "don't worry, for you the war is over, you are finished." They took about half a dozen of us to one side to the back of a hotel. I thought, "this is the end now against the wall and finished" but no, they kept us there for an hour or so while they went through the town. I found that the front line troops were gentlemen, they treated you as a soldier.' Guardsman Syd Pritchard. 11 Platoon, 4 Company, 2 Welsh Guards.[17]

Windsor-Lewis had nothing but praise for the stand his men had made.

'My little force had fought most splendidly in the face of heavy odds. Exhausted and without proper nourishment they never lost heart.' Major J C Windsor-Lewis, OC 3 Company, 2 Welsh Guards.[18]

Second Lieutenant Peter Hanbury's war had also come to end. He had been captured the previous day, on Friday 24 May. When he had woken that morning he had still harboured hopes of a fighting escape with his men even though he believed the French had surrendered and the Germans were all over the town. It was a forlorn hope. His diary, written soon after his arrival in a POW camp in Germany records the mixture of emotions he experienced on his capture.

'The Germans had taken complete possession of Boulogne and the French had surrendered in the Citadel. Our men were in good form – Peter and I had organised quite a decent breakfast and made every man wash, shave and clean his weapon. We replenished the SAA from an abandoned RAF lorry. I found some .38 ammunition for my revolver, the intention being to make a break that night. Then Jack and Henry's side shot a German bicyclist and that attracted two heavy tanks. They lumbered incredibly slowly up the road and then, with great deliberation, started to pump shells into "Jack's house". It was obviously hopeless, but Jack waited for interminable minutes before he surrendered. "Aus, Aus, Loss, Loss." Weary minutes in which we were searched until our arms almost broke...The four officers were separated out and put against a wall, and a tank turret turned to point a machine gun at us. At that moment a German officer arrived and shouted at the tank crew, and we were returned to the men. I really didn't care whether they shot us or not. I experienced a real relief not to feel one was the quarry of the Germans one could see on the hill from our look out. One of the German soldiers tried to pull off my signet ring but it was too tight...It was then that the bitterness of our position set in. We marched two miles to a field and halted. It was full of French. Spent the night with no protection in pouring rain...The men were marvellous and snuggled all round us to keep us warm.' Second Lieutenant Peter Hanbury. OC 12 Platoon, 4 Company, 2 Welsh Guards.[19]

Hanbury, Pritchard, Davies, Windsor-Lewis and many more were now 'in the bag'. Some, like the irrepressible Major Windsor-Lewis, would escape and go on to fight the Germans in other theatres. Most would spend the rest of the war in captivity. For these the battle for Boulogne was over and so, in effect, was the war. On the evening of 25 May Sergeant Arthur Evans, still in his hospital bed after having pieces of a grenade removed from his left ankle, noticed that all had become 'ominously quiet.' Evans was out of touch with what was happening in the town and couldn't have done anything about it even if he had been. His injuries would not allow it. The next morning Evans was surprised to see an immaculately turned out German officer accompanying the surgeons on their rounds.

'At the time my mind failed to comprehend the significance of his presence. Perhaps he had come to visit some German wounded? But no! This was my first day as a POW – only another one thousand eight hundred and eleven to go!' Sergeant Arthur Evans, 2 i/c Anti-Tank Platoon, 2 Irish Guards, Attached 20 Guards Brigade.[20]

1. Major J C Windsor-Lewis, OC 3 Company, 2 Welsh Guards. PRO CAB 106/228.
2. Guardsman Syd Pritchard. 11 Platoon, 4 Company, 2 Welsh Guards. Author's tape transcript.
3. *ibid.*
4. Guardsman Doug Davies. 8 Platoon, 3 Company, 2 Welsh Guards. Author's tape transcript.
5. *ibid.*
6. Guardsman Syd Pritchard. *op.cit.*
7. *Oberleutnant* Künzel. 'Einnahme von Boulogne-sur-Mer', in *Militär-Wochenblatt*, No.35, Cols. 1517-1521. (Berlin 1940)
9. Second Lieutenant Peter Hanbury. OC 12 Platoon, 4 Company, 2 Welsh Guards. *A Not Very Military Experience.*
9. Corporal Joseph Bryan. 2 Welsh Guards, attached 20 Guards Brigade Anti-Tank Company. Author's tape transcript.
10. *Oberleutnant* Dietz. 'Abbeville und Boulogne unter den Schlagen einer Panzerdivision', in Guderian H (Ed) *Mit den Panzern in Ost und West. Vol.1.*
11. *ibid.*
12. Corporal Joseph Bryan. *op.cit.*
13. Guardsman Doug Davies. *op.cit.*
14. Guardsman Syd Pritchard. *op.cit.*
15. Major J C Windsor-Lewis. *op.cit.*
16. Guardsman Doug Davies. *op.cit.*
17. Guardsman Syd Pritchard. *op.cit.*
18. Major J C Windsor-Lewis. *op.cit.*
19. Second Lieutenant Peter Hanbury. *op.cit.*
20. Sergeant. Arthur Evans, 2 i/c Anti-Tank Platoon, 2 Irish Guards. Attached 20 Guards Brigade. *Sojourn in Silesia.*

Headquarters,
20th Guards Brigade,
Roman Way Camp,
Colchester, Essex.

29th May, 1940.

Dear Admiral Ramsay,

I am writing to you on behalf of every
officer and man in this Brigade to express our
admiration and gratitude for the part played
by H.M. Destroyers in the evacuation from
Boulogne.

But for their skill and courage in action
I am certain that the evacuation would have resulted
in far higher casualties, and might well have
proved impossible. The debt which my Brigade
owe to the British Navy will not be forgotten, and
I can assure you that the way in which they performed
their duties will be remembered by us all.

I hope you will convey this message from the
20th Guards Brigade to the officers and men concerned,
and with it our sympathy for casualties sustained
during an action fought on our behalf.

Yours very sincerely,

Vice-Admiral B. H. Ramsay, C.B., M.V.O.,
Dover Castle,
DOVER, Kent.

Copy to:- 2 Irish Guards.
2 Welsh Guards.

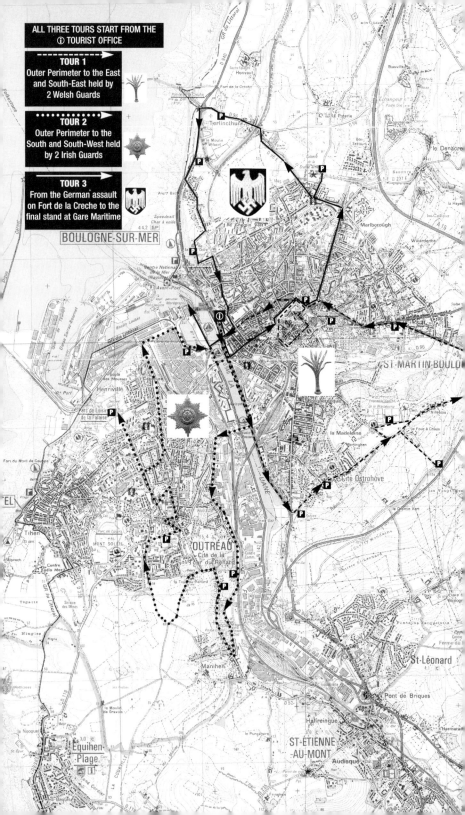

ALL THREE TOURS START FROM THE
ⓘ TOURIST OFFICE

TOUR 1
Outer Perimeter to the East
and South-East held by
2 Welsh Guards

TOUR 2
Outer Perimeter to the
South and South-West held
by 2 Irish Guards

TOUR 3
From the German assault
on Fort de la Creche to the
final stand at Gare Maritime

BOULOGNE-SUR-MER

TOUR 1

The Outer Perimeter to the East and South-East held by 2 Welsh Guards

Allow a day

This tour, which follows the line of the outer perimeter and the initial positions held by 2 Welsh Guards, whose task was to block and cover all routes into Boulogne from the East, has been set out as a tour by car due to the distances involved. There is no reason why it cannot be undertaken by cyclists or indeed keen walkers however, since a walk around the suggested route will provide insights into the distance travelled by some companies after disembarkation, all of it on foot. Indeed, 'walking the course' may well be the best way of understanding the difficulties faced by both officers and men in terms of the enormous front one infantry battalion was expected to cover.

From the Tourist Office at 24 Boulevard Gambetta follow signs for Le Touquet, Abbeville, Arras and Montreuil and **drive south on the D940, along the Boulevard de la Poste and the Boulevard Diderot, along the eastern bank of the River Liane.** This road turns into the Boulevard d'Alembert after approximately two kilometres. **Continue until the road merges with the D96**, the Route de Paris at a major junction. **Take the left hand lane following the signs for Ostrohove and Centre Sportif de la Waroquerie and turn left across the carriageway taking the road directly in front named the rue Apolline. Follow the road up the hill and park the car** with care on the raised pavement just after the road bends to the left. **Leave the car and retrace your tracks to the junction of the D940 and the D96.**

This is the road to St. Leonard and Samer covered by two platoons of 2 Company, 2 Welsh Guards under the command of Major Cas Jones-Mortimer on the afternoon of 22 May 1940. His task was to block and cover the road to Samer and he established his HQ in a house near a railway bridge, now demolished, some 250 metres from the junction back towards Boulogne along the Route de Paris.

2 Company, along with 4 Company, had originally been ordered to march out to

The junction of the D940 with the D96 near Ostrohove. The Pont de Pittendal is in the dip. Here the road was cratered by the Royal Engineers rupturing a gas main.

a rendezvous in the village of St. Leonard, two kilometres from where you are standing, out along the D940 towards Samer from where they marched to take up their positions on the outer perimeter. Note how the road falls away to the Pont de Pitendal which crosses the Ruisseau de la Fontaine de Bourreau stream as you look to the south and then rises on the other side of the Ravin de Pitendal. The road here was cratered just in front of the Welsh Guards' posts by the Royal Engineers to assist in the defence of the perimeter. The explosions ruptured a gas main from which flames belched forth continuously; their fierce glow clearly illuminating the immediate vicinity as darkness fell.

Retrace your steps back uphill along the rue Apolline towards the heart of 2 Company's positions. Note the terrain to your right beyond the houses and particularly how the ground falls away sharply to the stream below and then rises on the other side of the valley. The high ground is the long shoulder of Mont Lambert, the summit of which lies three kilometres to the north-east. The A16 Autoroute now runs along the top of the Mont Lambert ridge following almost exactly the route of the 1940 road through the hamlet of le Chemin Vert. The Welsh Guards of 2 Company saw German armoured vehicles patrolling the ridge during the evening of 22 May.

It is clear that some of the steeper slopes on this eastern sector were not ideal for the German armour but roads and tracks still snake down from the Mont Lambert spur, just as they did in 1940, at several points further up the valley where the slopes are less steep. These access points were not easy to defend given the nature of the terrain and the fact that fire positions were not linked, leaving 'dead ground' between companies, platoons and sections due to their being stretched along the front in this sector.

Return to the car and drive on up the Rue Apolline. The first turn on the right, the Rue Bel Air, was the approximate site of an anti-tank gun, one of three which were deployed on the forward slopes of the ravine to the east to cover the roads and tracks into the village of Ostrohove. **Drive on until the road bends slightly to the left and at this point take the road off to the left called the Rue du Mont d'Ostrohove.** There is ample parking in the Place de l'Orme just behind the annexe to the Mairie on the main road.

Another platoon of 2 Company were responsible for defending the roads leading to the village but the defence of the village itself was the responsibility of HQ Company under the command of Captain R B Hodgkinson. Lieutenant Colonel Stanier set up his first battalion HQ in the schoolhouse in the north-west corner of the square during the afternoon of 22 May 1940. In 2001 the building was still in use as a school. Sometime around 9.00 pm on 22 May, Stanier moved his HQ back about 400 metres along the Rue du Mont d'Ostrohove to a cottage at a waterworks near a light railway line, all of which have long since disappeared. It was whilst Stanier was at this cottage that he became embroiled in an argument with the French manager of the waterworks. Returning late, tired and hungry from inspecting his battalion's positions on the night of 22 May, Stanier was greeted by his second in command, Major John Vigor and his Adjutant Captain Robin Rose-Price, who told him that the French manager of the waterworks was incensed about burly guardsmen trampling all over his flower and rose beds. He was waiting to see Stanier. At that point a huge explosion rocked the cottage and everyone ducked to avoid what they thought were German artillery rounds. In fact the HQ petrol cooker had exploded along with Stanier's supper. Quartermaster Bray threw a feather mattress on the cooker to extinguish the flames which produced such odious fumes that the British had to don their gas masks. The French manager, bereft of a mask, fled coughing and spluttering from the cottage, never to be seen again.

Walk to the east side of the Place d'Orme and rejoin the main road which has now become the Rue de l'Orme. Before leaving the square remember that the Germans had attacked 2 and 3 Companies at 7.30 am on 23 May and by 11.00 am 2 Company had been in action for three-and-a-half hours. German artillery registered accurately on the light railway 300 metres or so to your rear from about 9.00 am and one platoon of 2 Company suffered as a result. As further attacks fell on 2 Company – and on HQ Company in positions close to where you are standing – Lieutenant Colonel Stanier's company commanders warned him of the strong possibility of encirclement. Stanier decided to readjust his line by moving back 300 – 400 metres to the north-east to the line of houses on the Rue Henri Malo. This was behind the light railway, parts of which are now a footpath on the line of the Rue du Tir a l'Arc. Before this re-adjustment was complete Stanier received orders to withdraw further back towards the town. Note also that a second anti-tank gun was sited a little way down the forward slope of the valley at a point opposite the junction of the Rue Apolline and the Rue du Mont d'Ostrohove.

Turn left and after 100 metres or so you will see a 'no through road' sign off to your right. This is the Rue Patin and down this road was the site of the third anti-tank gun covering the approaches to Ostrohove. This track was the only one marked on the maps issued to 20 Brigade HQ which linked Ostrohove with the road along the crest of the Mont Lambert spur on the other side of the valley. The road forks after a short distance and the tracks now lead to private houses.

Return to the car and continue to drive up the hill along the Rue de l'Orme towards the village of St Martin-Boulogne. The buildings on either side of the road begin to thin out after 500 metres or so. Note how the ground drops away steeply to your immediate right. The terrain here has not changed much from 1940 apart from the intrusion of the Autoroute along the crest of the ridge. Note also how the ground rises to your left towards la Madeleine. **After another 250-300 metres take the road which bears sharp left up the hill onto the Rue du Four a Chaux. Turn right after another 250 metres** as the road levels out and **park in front of the sports ground** a little way down this road on your left. **Leave the car and retrace your tracks back to the junction. Turn left and walk down the slope until the Rue du Four a Chaux meets the main road.**

The Rue Patin. A third anti-tank gun covered this approach into Ostrohove.

You are now standing on the extremity of the right flank of the sector held by 3 Company under the command of Major Jim Windsor-Lewis. 3 Company's initial rendezvous had been the village of Ostrohove but Windsor-Lewis was ordered to move further 'to the left' and hold the line from Ostrohove as far as the crossroads north-west of Mont Lambert. The right flank here was held by 7 platoon under Second Lieutenant Hesketh (Hexey) Hughes with posts covering the knot of roads and tracks around the small hamlets of la Madeleine and Varoquerie – now shown on maps as Waroquerie – a little further along the road to the north-east. Turn left onto the main

165

The road junction at la Madeleine, held by sections of Second Lieutenant Hexey Hughes' 7 Platoon, 3 Company.

road and walk on until you come to a small group of houses on the corner of a junction with a road to your right. This road crosses the valley and passes under the A16 Autoroute on its way to the villages of Echingen and Questinghen and eventually the town of Desvres. It was one of the routes taken by German armour of Combat Group Prittwitz after they had captured Desvres. Note from the map how an unimpeded advance by this route could take tanks to within spitting distance of the harbour in the heart of the town.

In 1940 la Madeleine consisted of little more than four small houses, two cottages and an *estaminet* clustered around the road junction. Second Lieutenant Hexey Hughes was in position at a post just south-west of the junction when his isolated platoon was attacked by four German tanks coming down the road from Echingen at around 10.30 am on the morning of 23 May under cover of an artillery and mortar barrage.

Hughes had managed to dig one anti-tank gun in to cover the junction with some success and he had another to the rear. One tank advanced towards the junction and moved north across the gentler slopes behind the estaminet. Note how the ground to the north of the road to Echingen is far less steep and rugged than that to the south. A second tank knocked out Hughes' second anti-tank gun and soon he noticed two more working their way around him. He reasoned that he would soon be surrounded so he decided to withdraw his men to the other side of the road to obtain a better line of fire. The decision proved fatal for Hughes and

some of his men who were killed as they moved out of cover and crossed the open ground.

Walk on and then take the next sharp left which will complete a rough triangular circuit taking you back to your car parked at the sports ground.

Retrace your tracks, driving south-west, and turn left at the junction. Turn left at the main road and then first right onto the narrow road to Echingen. **Drive up to the top of the slope and park the car before the motorway underpass.** Turn around and look at the panorama of Boulogne laid out in front of you. This is a panzer crewman's eye view of the positions of 2 Welsh Guards on the line of the road running along the western slopes of the ravine at the

The road east towards Echingen.

bottom of the hill and also of the ultimate prize in the distance – Boulogne. Note the line of the road as it snakes down towards Hexey Hughes' position at the bottom of the hill and then follow it up and over the ridge through la Madeleine on its way into the town. From here on a clear day one can see the docks and, further to the right, the unmistakable dome of the nineteenth century Basilique de Notre Dame in the medieval walled Haute Ville. Further right still on the horizon one can make out the rectangular outline of the church tower in the village of St. Martin which was held by 4 Company. Look closely and between these two landmarks one can make out the Colonne de la Grande Armée topped by the figure of Napoleon Bonaparte. Scanning the horizon still further to the right will bring your eye to the radio masts on top of Mont Lambert which overlooked the positions of two sections of 8 platoon of 3 Company under Second Lieutenant Ralph Pilcher. Half left, on the high ground beyond the docks and the western bank of the River Liane, lies the village of Outreau and the south western perimeter held by 2 Irish Guards. From this vantage point the almost impossible task handed to 20 Brigade can be appreciated.

Head back down the hill and turn right at the junction towards Mont Lambert along the road which has now become the Rue de la Croix Abot. Two sections of 8 platoon of 3 Company were spread out along this road up to the junction with the present D341 the Rue de Desvres, (beware, the road to St. Omer a little further north is also numbered D 341 on the IGN map just to confuse the issue!). **Follow the road keeping Mont Lambert to your right as far as the junction with the D 341.**The wartime junction has now disappeared to make way for the cutting of the motorway interchange.

The new road deviates slightly to the west before joining the main road at this busy junction. Parking is a little difficult here so **turn left at the junction and drive west towards St. Martin for 250 metres or so.** There is ample parking outside one of the large new buildings on your right. **Leave the car and walk east up the slight rise back towards the junction.**

Major Windsor-Lewis deployed two sections of Pilcher's 8 platoon to cover the crossroads which would have been where the present day overpass now straddles the motorway. As you walk towards the junction and leave the buildings behind note how the ground opens up into a hollow on your left. It was in a farm house on approximately this spot that Major Windsor-Lewis had his 3 Company HQ with two anti-tank guns a little further forward in the hollow to your left. It was whilst he was here on his rounds that Lieutenant Colonel Stanier peered over a wall and saw three German tanks come bursting out of the village of Mont Lambert – the houses of which you can see beyond the motorway bridge up the road in front of you – at around 7.30 am on the morning of 23 May and started firing at the men holding the cross roads and the anti-tank guns which were just in the hollow to your left. Note the house on your right. This house is on the site of a cottage which was held by Windsor-Lewis's 9 platoon being held in reserve on that morning.

Walk on to the junction of the road you have just driven up from Ostrohove. In front of you stood a monument to the south of the crossroads close to which Second Lieutenant Ralph Pilcher had set up his platoon HQ. To the north of the crossroads were two more sections of 8 Platoon.

Although the road layout has changed, imagine the men of 8 Platoon like Doug Davies and Arthur Boswell dug into one and two-man foxholes to the north and south of the road a little way ahead of you. These men were at the apex of the Welsh line, which described a rough arrowhead pointing to the east and they felt

167

the full force of the German blow, which started with a fusillade of machine gun fire accompanying the tank attack.

One of the tanks set fire to the makeshift barricade blocking the road with machine gun fire and at one point stopped so close to Second Lieutenant Neil Perrins commanding 9 platoon, who was out on patrol at the time, that he was able to stand next to it undetected! Captain Hamil Carter was wounded in the arm whilst in position just to the left of the crossroads. Even as late as the evening of 23 May during the evacuation Lieutenant Colonel Stanier, who had been told about Carter's wound, thought that he had been evacuated. At that time Stanier thought that his battalion would be surrounded and captured and that Carter would be able to tell those at home all about what had happened but Carter had been taken to hospital in Boulogne and was still there when the Germans came. He was unable to write with his damaged arm for the rest of his life. The men of 8 Platoon were ordered to withdraw as best they could as they were in danger of being surrounded and some escaped under machine gun fire in the direction of the motorway to the north.

It was also at this time that anti-tank guns manned by Sergeant Green and Corporal Joseph Bryan, sited around 3 Company HQ in the hollow you have just passed on your left, made a spirited response to the tank threat, putting at least one out of action.

Return to the car and drive west along the D 341 towards the buildings of St. Martin. Turn right after 500 metres – you cannot go straight on due to the one-way system in operation – and **then turn left at the traffic lights at the next major junction,** the Route de St. Omer. **Drive on until you see the church tower and take the left turn immediately after the church. Turn right immediately into the public car park**. You are now in the Place d'Hotel de Ville in the heart of the village of St. Martin-Boulogne. Note the proximity of the Hotel de Ville and the church.

St. Martin was held by the men of 4 Company under Captain Jack Higgon from 22-23 May 1940. Their task was to secure the northern flank of the perimeter along the Desvres road (the D 341) from 3 Company HQ as far as the church in St. Martin itself by blocking all roads leading from the north. This would also mean that the route to St. Omer was blocked.

Leave the car and walk towards the church. The centre of the village has been re developed but it was in this area that Guardsman Syd Pritchard went to wash himself at the village pump early on the morning of 23 May and saw a German spotter plane circle above 4 Company positions. The German attack started soon afterwards.

Head for the church, taking the road to your right, the Rue de Desvres and **walk for some 500-600 metres until you come to a crossroads with traffic lights. Take the road to your right** the Rue Giraux Sannier. **Walk a little way down the hill and then stop near the bend where the road overlooks the valley of St Martin.** From this vantage point it is possible to see right across the valley to the line of the road defended by 3 Company. Second Lieutenant Peter Hanbury's platoon, which included Guardsman Charles Thompson, was originally dug in on the slopes of the valley to your left. In 1940 the light railway wound its way up the far side of the valley from Ostrohove and would have passed the spot where you are standing on its way towards the church at St Martin. Several patrols went out into the valley during the evening and night of 22 May. At 10.30 pm Hanbury set out on a patrol of the valley which headed out along the line of the railway then circled round to your right almost as far as the church before coming back to his position along the ground behind you. He and his men expected to run into

Above: the church of St Martin with the top of its tower shot off. Right: the same view today.

Germans but the only living things encountered were rats scuttling around on a rubbish heap which startled his men.

Retrace your steps back towards the church. Hanbury was ordered to occupy new positions in the centre of St. Martin near the church after 'stand to' on the morning of 23 May. He established his HQ in the building on the corner of the Route de St. Omer and the Place J Moulin. The exterior of this building, now a bar and billiards room called *Le Regent*, has been substantially altered in recent years. Before the alterations it was still possible to see marks to the left of the doorway on the corner made by bullets which, Peter Hanbury felt, had been fired by a sniper in the church tower. He was not alone in thinking this. Guardsman Charles Thompson, one of Hanbury's platoon, recalled firing at a sniper hiding, 'behind the parapet of the church tower' at the time he was wounded. Hanbury decided to investigate and began to climb the stairs leading to the tower when the local priest pulled him down. He went back to his men and ordered Guardsman Bartlett and another man to neutralise the fire with two Bren guns. They claimed to have seen a rifle drop from the tower. Other accounts record that Cyril Heber-Percy, the commanding officer of 1 Company, which had moved up to block all the roads around and to the north of the church on the left of 4 Company at around 3.30 pm on 22 May, dug up some railway sleepers with the aid of Second Lieutenant Peter Black and elevated an anti-tank gun on them. It is recorded that they blew the top off the tower although there is no mention of any bodies ever having been recovered.

Enter the St. Martin Communal Cemetery extension, which is off the Rue Francois Boulanger opposite the church and **walk through the civilian cemetery**, past some hedges and down some steps to the far south-west corner. There are twenty-two Commonwealth War Graves here, twelve of which are the graves of Welsh Guardsmen killed in action during the fighting on the outer perimeter. The body of Second Lieutenant Hexey Hughes lies here in Row E, Grave 2, as does that of Doug Davies' friend Doug Morton in Row B, Grave 3, their final resting place forever looking out over the valley and the ground towards Mont Lambert and la Madeleine on which they fought and died.

Return to the car and follow the one-way system east past the church and then turn left and left again onto the Route de St. Omer coming back on yourself in an anti-clockwise circuit. Pass the church and drive down the hill towards Boulogne. This road follows the line of the withdrawal of 1, 3 and 4 Companies towards Boulogne during the afternoon of 23 May. **Drive on until you come to a signpost indicating a left turn marked Abbeville, Arras, Le Touquet, Montreuil and Stade de Libération** which also shows a distinctive green and white Commonwealth War Graves Commission (CWGC) sign. **Follow the Rue Framery and turn first left into the Rue de Dringhen and park the car** near the entrance to the southern section of the Cimetière de Est to your right. This is a large

Ex-Guardsman Syd Pritchard, 4 Coy, 2 Welsh Guards, returns to Boulogne (1999) to pay his respects to those of his comrades who fell in the fighting in May 1940.

civil cemetery, which lies just beyond the eastern corner of the Haute Ville. The CWGC cemetery forms a long narrow strip along the western edge of the southern section of the civil cemetery and is easily identified by locating the Cross of Sacrifice. Begun during the First World War when Boulogne

The bar known as le Regent in the village square of St Martin. This building, recently refurbished, was the HQ of Second Lieutenant Peter Hanbury on the morning of 23 May.

was one of the three main base ports used by the BEF, the cemetery holds almost 6,000 1914-18 graves and 200 casualties from 1939-45 are commemorated, including Welsh and Irish Guardsmen killed in the Boulogne fighting of 1940. Guardsman Brynmor Pugh, killed in action between the bogey wheels of a railway ambulance carriage during the final stand at the Gare Maritime on 24 May, was a comrade of Syd Pritchard. His body lies in Plot 13, Row C, Grave 16. Captain John Duncan also lies here in a grave next but one to that of Pugh (Plot 13, Row C, Grave 18). Duncan was killed by a bomb which burst close to him, Lieutenant Colonel Alexander Stanier and the padre as all three sheltered together under a railway truck on the quayside just prior to the evacuation of the battalion on the evening of 23 May. Stanier and the padre got up, Duncan didn't. Stanier later recalled that the twenty-eight year old, 'must have been killed by the shock'. Other graves belonging to members of the Pioneer Corps, RAMC, Royal Signals, Royal Engineers and the Royal Artillery killed in action between 23-25 May bear witness to the contribution of those units in the defence of Boulogne.

Return to the car and drive straight on up the Rue Dringhen turning left almost at the top and then left again at the junction with the main road. Drive back towards town and take a left turn at the next major junction onto the Rue Porte Neuve. You are now following the route taken by German troops during the morning of 24 May as they advanced to lay siege to the Citadel of the Haute Ville held by French forces under General Lanquetot commanding 21 Infantry Division. The area was known as 'Le Dernier Sou' in 1940 after a cabaret bar which stood nearby. Note the Porte Neuve otherwise known as the Porte de Calais and the thirteenth century walls of the Citadel to your front. Note also the imposing domed edifice of the Basilique Notre Dame. Drive towards the old walls and turn right into the car park just before the gate itself.

The medieval walled town is well worth a visit in itself as it has much to offer the visitor historically above and beyond the scope of the 1940 battle as well as being an atmospheric location for a lunch or coffee stop.

It is possible to walk the 1,400 metres along the top of the ramparts which were themselves built on the ancient remains of earlier Gallo-Roman walls between 1227 and 1231, taking in the four main gates and the seventeen towers along the way. This walk is rewarded by some stunning views of the surrounding countryside from the vantage point of the ramparts near the Porte des Degres, particularly to the south and the high ground beyond Outreau from which direction came the southern German Assault Group. From here the great strength of the walled citadel can be appreciated. Little wonder that the walls resisted wave after wave of German

The area known as 'Le Dernier Sou' taken from the Porte de Calais after the battle.

attacks and a battering by artillery, mortars and heavy flak guns from just after lunchtime on 24 May until they were finally breached in the early morning of 25 May after two German 88mm flak guns were brought up to fire at the walls at point blank range. One of the guns fired on the walls a little way down the hill from the Porte de Calais along the Boulevard August Mariette whilst the other fired from a point round the corner near the Rue Flahaut just north of the Porte des Dunes on the western wall. Also, a little way down from the Rue Flahaut opposite the ramparts you will see a row of houses. It was in a house along this row that Brigadier Fox-Pitt set up his first HQ.

Whilst standing near the the Porte de Calais and just in front of the Cathedral, note that German storming parties used a ladder which – according to General Heinz Guderian himself – had been taken from the kitchen of a nearby house to scale what remained of the ramparts and finally broke into the Citadel. Note also that the 300 or so exhausted defenders of the ancient Château built in 1231 by Philippe Hurepel, Count of Boulogne, marched out of this gate at 10.30 on 25 May under the admiring gaze of *Oberstleutnant* Decker commanding 2 Schützen

Now: the same view today.

Regiment who was fulsome in his praise of their heroic resistance. These men under the command of *Commandant* Berriat, had defended the Château oblivious to the fact that Lanquetot had given the order for the garrison to surrender some two hours earlier. It was only after a message from Lanquetot himself got through that the men in the Château finally laid down their arms.

Walk through the Porte de Calais and turn take the second left onto the Rue de Château and then on to the Château itself. The ramparts in this corner were held by infantry under Lieutenant Colonel Santini and the remnants of 13 Regiment Regionale under Colonel Wimet who had fought their way up to the Haute Ville on 23 May. The Château itself; a masterpiece of medieval military architecture, complete with underground passages, was held by Berriat's men and its great strength helped the French garrison resist the German onslaught until ordered to surrender by General Lanquetot.

The Château also has a special connection with British military history in that the body of Britain's Unknown Warrior rested overnight in its chapel, the Chapelle Ardente, on 8 November 1920 on its way from St. Pol to its final resting place in Westminster Abbey two days later. On 9 November the body of the Unknown Warrior was taken from the chapel and left the Citadel via the Porte de Calais on its way to the Quai Gambetta drawn in a French army wagon followed on foot by the then Adjutant General Sir George Macdonagh and Marshal Foch. The body was then transported across the channel aboard the destroyer HMS *Verdun*, a ship specially chosen in honour of the French sacrifice in defending that town.

It is also interesting to note that the Château was used as a prison after the Second World War up until 1974. Today it is a museum housing the town's important collection of exhibits including Gallo Roman, Greek and Egyptian relics. (Telephone: 00 33 321 10 02 20 for details of opening times – closed on Tuesdays.)

After exploring the architectural gems of the Haute Ville **return to the car, turn left out of the car park and follow the road system towards the Pont Marguet and the harbour via the Rue Dutertre and the Rue Faidherbe. Park along the front near the Quai Gambetta,** (pay and display), which in 1940 had many more buildings along the quayside including the customs house and the area where Doug Davies first sheltered behind a dustbin after his withdrawal from 3 Company positions near Mont Lambert. It is worth a **walk back along the quay heading south to the Pont de l'Entente Cordiale and turning left onto the main road,** the Rue de la Lampe, **back into town and uphill towards the Grand Rue. After passing the third street on your right,** the Rue Nationale you will come to St Nicolas' church in the Place Dalton. It was in this square that Sergeant Arthur Evans of 2 Irish Guards and his comrades of an anti-tank platoon attached to 20 Brigade formed up after disembarkation on 22 May, Evans went in search of food and walked round the back of a restaurant in the south east corner of the square. The restaurant, *Chez Alfred*, is still there. Evans got no food and returning to Place Dalton found it empty of men. After hitching a ride on a lorry heading for Calais he was finally reunited with his men by mid-afternoon not long before the Germans attacked the Irish Guards positions in Outreau. There is a market in the Place Dalton on Wednesday and Saturday mornings. **Walk back down the Grand Rue to the car parked on the Quai Gambetta to complete the tour.**

TOUR 2

The Outer Perimeter to the South and South West held by 2 Irish Guards

Allow a day

This tour, which follows the line of the outer perimeter and the initial positions held by 2 Irish Guards, whose task was to block and cover all routes into Boulogne from the south and south-west has, like Tour 1, been set out as a tour by car due to the distances involved. Again there is no reason why keen cyclists or walkers cannot undertake it however, and again 'getting out on the ground' either by cycle or on foot will provide a unique appreciation of the terrain covered by the Irish Guards during their initial deployment and subsequent withdrawal. Tracing the Irish Guards line today takes the visitor from unlovely industrial zones close to the banks of the Liane out onto exposed undulating upland and then on towards the coast overlooking the Petit Port, Boulogne's second harbour near Le Portel. It is a tour in complete contrast to Tour 1.

From the Tourist Office at 24 Boulevard Gambetta **drive south on the D940**, the Boulevard de la Poste and the Boulevard Diderot, **along the eastern bank of the River Liane until you approach the new bridge over the River Liane,** the Viaduc Jean-Jacques Rousseau. **Take the right hand lane and drive up the ramp taking the exit before the underpass and turn right following signs for Abbeville, Arras, Le Touquet, Montreuil and Z I de la Liane to go over the bridge. Take the left lane as you approach the roundabout and turn left onto the Boulevard Montesquieu signposted 'Outreau, Centre Salengro, Garromanche, Equihen Plage, Camping.'** At the traffic lights the road ahead splits into three. **Take the extreme left lane onto the D52**, the Rue Roger Salengro. This is the lower approach road into Boulogne. **Drive under the railway bridge past some terraced cottages on your left and an apartment block next to the road on your right. Follow the road as it bends to the right** and you will begin to pass a wooded bank to your right with the railway close by on your left. After some 400 metres or so the wooded bank ends and a concealed drive, signed 'no through road' heads uphill at right angles to the road. It is possible to **park with care here** on the raised verge on the right hand side of the road.

This was the site of two of the anti-tank guns of Eardley-Wilmot's anti-tank platoon under the command of Sergeant Arthur Evans. Evans's task, as second in

The view down the road towards Manihen. Sergeant Arthur Evans would have observed in this direction in May 1940.

command of the platoon, was to cover the low road which led into the village of Outreau and Boulogne beyond. Note how the road, one of only four which led through Outreau into Boulogne, is hemmed in by the steep sided ridge to the west and the railway and the river to the east. If the Germans wished to approach Boulogne by this route their armour would by necessity become funnelled down this road with little room for manoeuvre once on it. Note also the bend in the road some 200 metres ahead which would have helped to conceal the location of Evans's anti-tank weapons from the advancing panzers. Sergeant Evans eventually rejoined his men at this spot after being split up from them just after disembarkation. He arrived in position not long before the Germans launched their first assault on the forward platoon of 1 Company just in advance of his position towards the village of Manihen a short distance round the bend.

The men of 1 Company under Captain Conolly McCausland had arrived in Boulogne later than their comrades after sailing on a later boat and had barely begun to break the ground to dig their trenches on the left flank of the Irish line when the Germans hit them at around 3.30 pm on the afternoon of 22 May. By 5.30 pm German field artillery brought onto the high ground you can see in the distance began to shell the Irish positions and down the road behind the barrage came the leading tank of *Oberleutnant* Rudolf Behr's platoon.

Arthur Evans heard 'the distinct rumbling of tanks' and then saw Behr's leading tank round the bend with the commander upright in the turret looking through binoculars. Evans ordered his team to open fire and they hit the tank with two rounds as the crew baled out and abandoned the panzer. A bullet struck and killed the wireless operator as he made his escape. He was one of four killed and six wounded from Behr's platoon during the afternoon of 22 May.

The fighting in and amongst the back gardens and hedgerows beyond the patch of open ground in front of you and up the bank towards the houses on the ridge to your right was a chaotic and confused affair, which dragged on intermittently all afternoon as the Germans tried to break 1 Company's grip on the left flank. Towards 10.00 pm the Germans sent dismounted motorcycle infantry in against Evans's guns but these were harassed by accurate and disciplined fire from Irish positions in amongst woodland to your rear. Eventually a platoon on the right got near enough to toss hand grenades in amongst Evans's crew and Evans was knocked to the ground. Realising the gravity of the situation Evans ordered his men to withdraw back towards the town after first disabling the guns. He later realised he had been wounded in the ankle and was taken to a hospital in Boulogne where he was captured when the Germans finally took the town.

Return to the car and continue along the D52 into the village of Manihen. **Turn sharp right when you see signs for Outreau and the D235 and drive uphill.** You will pass a green information board signed 'Outreau' on your left and some iron railings on your right. If you look right you will see the industrial areas in the valley below whilst the ground to the left continues to rise. **Look out for a row of roadside houses on your left as you approach a wooded area to your right front. There are parking bays opposite the houses. Park the car here.**

On a clear day this point offers a superb view across the valley of the Liane and a different perspective of the initial positions of 2 Company, 2 Welsh Guards in and around Ostrohove, the village across the valley to the north-east. Note the A16 motorway snaking across the slopes of the valley opposite and up towards Mont Lambert, the highest point in the distance. Note the large house across the valley opposite. Scan to the left and you will see the golden arches of a McDonald's; a

View across the valley of the River Liane, from Outreau. The village centre left is Ostrohove, held by 2 Company, 2 Welsh Guards. Note Mont Lambert to the right.

little to the left again note another road which runs up through the village of Ostrohove. This was the line of a platoon of 2 Company, 2 Welsh Guards with anti-tank guns covering the approaches to the village from the east and south-east. Scan the horizon to the left. Note the church tower of St. Martin and further left still the distinctive dome of the Cathedral of Notre Dame in the Haute Ville.

Drive on taking the 90° left turn after some 200 metres and follow the road as it bends sharp right. Turn sharp left – almost back onto yourself – after a few metres and drive uphill onto a narrow one-way road. As you breast the rise and reach the junction at the top you will notice a road leading off to your left. **Turn left and park the car carefully** as soon as it is safe to do so - the roads are narrow here and large farm machinery does tend to move at speed around the corners.

This area is known as la Tour de Renard and you are now in position on the left flank of that part of the perimeter held by the men of 4 Company, 2 Irish Guards. **Leave the car and walk out along the road to the south towards some grassy domes a few hundred metres distant.** You are now walking towards the advanced positions held by the forward platoon of 4 Company under the command of Lieutenant Peter Reynolds. His sections held the ridge here around the reservoirs (the ones you see here are of postwar construction) and a trigonometrical point, the site of which has moved some 300 metres further on and to the left of the road from that marked on the maps issued in 1940!

When the Germans attacked on the morning of 23 May they began by assaulting 1 Company as they had done the previous day but then quickly switched the point of attack onto Captain Murphy's 4 Company, concentrating particularly on the forward platoon led by Reynolds. Look down the road and note how the ground undulates beyond the reservoirs giving rise to patches of 'dead ground' with hidden folds and hollows to the south-west. In some places where the ground falls away from the summit to the west behind and to your right, 4 Company's posts were below the level of the surrounding hills.

Reflect here on the open nature of the terrain and how control of the ridge and the surrounding high ground would allow the Germans to observe movements in the village of Outreau behind you. Note also how exposed this position must have seemed as the men first heard the sounds of firing drift up the ridge from 1

Company positions to the east and then found themselves bearing the brunt of the German assault as machine gun fire, shells and mortar rounds rained down on them at around 7.45 am. When the shelling lifted the panzers moved in to isolate the platoon and for more than an hour the Irish fought steel plate with rifle bullets. The situation was precarious when up one of the roads to your rear marched Lieutenant Simon Leveson with the leading section of his carrier platoon in order to reinforce Reynolds. He had been on his way to reinforce 1 Company but felt Reynolds was more in need of help at that time. By 8.45 am Captain Murphy felt his only option was to withdraw Reynolds's men immediately if they were to be saved but by then it was too late; Reynolds and Leveson were surrounded. Captain Murphy and Captain Reid tried to reach them several times but on each occasion the hail of fire sweeping the hillsides beat them back. There was no doubt in Captain Murphy's mind that any further attempt to reach them meant certain death. Both Peter Reynolds and Simon Leveson were killed in action here and only nineteen men out of 107 from 4 Company were present when the roll was called on their return to England.

Retrace your steps to the car. Note the proximity of the Channel coast over the fields to your left and the village of Le Portel which was held by 3 Company throughout the battle. **On reaching the car continue to drive south past the reservoirs along the narrow metalled road until you reach a crossroads. Turn sharp right onto the 'one-way' road leading back into Outreau. Stop on the verge after some 500 metres** and keep at least two wheels on the metalled surface in very wet conditions. Look out over the fields to the clumps of trees and bushes to your right. From this vantage point you can appreciate the fields of fire of the German machine-gunners as they set up their weapons overlooking some of Reynolds' posts at the Tour du Renard during the fighting on the morning of 23 May.

Continue downhill until the road becomes a two-lane carriageway again and drive on until you arrive at a main crossroads with a school on the corner. Turn right onto the Rue Kennedy. Look out for a Union Jack flying up ahead on your left and after 200 metres or so you will see the entrance to a cemetery on the roadside to your left. Drive a little way past the cemetery and park in the car park on the left opposite a football stadium.

This is the communal cemetery of Outreau and the small CWGC plot, in the middle of the churchyard to the eastern side, is clearly identified by the presence of the Union flag. This quiet spot is the last resting place of most of the Irish Guards killed in the Battle for Boulogne – seventeen of the graves here are those of Guardsmen. The bodies of the twenty-four-year-old Lieutenant Peter Reynolds (whose father Douglas, a father he never knew, was awarded the VC for his actions at Le Cateau and Pysloup during August and September 1914. He died in 1916) and the twenty-two-year-old Lieutenant Simon Leveson lie here. Interestingly a number of the Irish Guards graves show the date of death as being between 23 May to 4 June; presumably the dates on which the men were last seen alive and the date on which their bodies were finally recovered. Two of the graves are of unknown soldiers and one of these belongs to an unknown soldier of the Royal Ulster Rifles killed in action in May 1940.

Leave the cemetery and return to the car. Turn left out of the car park and then take the left turn signposted Le Portel, Centre Ville. There is a one-way system in operation around the centre of Outreau so you have to drive on, crossing cobbles and past the Mairie on the Rue du Biez. **You must turn left at the sign for**

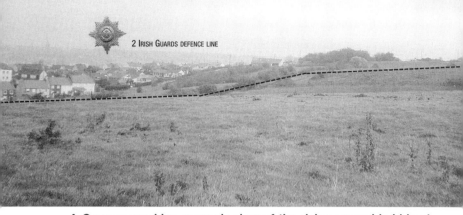

A German machine-gunner's view of the rising ground held by 4 Company, 2 Irish Guards around la Tour de Renard.

'Parking' in the Place Beregovoy onto the Rue Jules Michelet. At the next crossroads turn sharp right onto the Rue Auguste Comte.
This area around the centre of Outreau was part of the new line held by men of the depleted 4 Company after they had withdrawn from their outer positions in and around la Tour de Renard. Lieutenant Colonel Haydon decided to readjust his line at around 9.00 am as both the forward platoons of 1 and 4 Companies had been all but destroyed as fighting units. Haydon's new line approximated the line of the subterranean railway line which follows the Avé Maria railway tunnel. 1 Company held buildings near the present day École de Danse and the Centre Culturel Phénix covering the road leading down the hill into Boulogne and the road leading to Battalion HQ which was located near the present site of the 'Ateliers Municipaux' yard on the Rue Jean Jaures. 4 Company arrived in the area you have just driven through on their right flank at around 9.45 am after heavy fighting during the withdrawal.

Drive straight on until you come to a crossroads at the junction with the Rue Carnot. This is the approximate line of the junction between 2 and 3

'Some corner of a foreign field.' Irish Guards killed in the fighting of 23 May rest in Outreau Communal Cemetery.

Companies during the initial deployment on 22 May. From this point the road becomes the Avenue des Canadiens, so named in honour of the liberators of Boulogne in September 1944. You are now driving in the rear of 2 Company positions after Captain Madden had pulled his left flank back to conform with the withdrawal of 4 Company to his left. Drive further and cross another crossroads onto the Rue J P Gachere towards the Serres Municipals and park in the Parc de Loisirs de la Falaise. Park the car and walk out along the path towards the coast.

You are now slightly to the rear of the extreme right flank of the Irish Guards initial positions held by 3 Company which was not attacked directly during 23 May and held its line all day until the order came for the final withdrawal to the harbour. 3 Company's task was to hold the village of Le Portel and block the approaches to Boulogne along the coast and the roads from Etaples.

Walk towards the south until you reach a point overlooking the now disused hovercraft port. It is interesting to note the contrast between the terrain here on the coast and that around the Tour de Renard held by Lieutenant Reynolds and, further east, the positions of Sergeant Evans near Manihen. From this point on the cliffs above the coast you have a good view of the second of Boulogne's ports. Note the opening to the Avé Maria Rail Tunnel in the side of the cliff near the hoverport. You are now standing on the extreme right flank of the Irish line, the Guardsmen would have dug their trenches and foxholes on the cliff tops in this area with a good view of the coast below and the cliffs of the headland to your front.

Return to the car and retrace your tracks back along the Rue J P Gachere and the Avenue des Canadiens to the third crossroads which is the junction with the Rue Carnot. In 1940 this road linked Boulogne with Le Portel. Another of Eardley-Wilmot's anti-tank guns was deployed on the right flank with 3 Company although its position is not shown on the Brigade map. It was probably deployed somewhere in this vicinity as the Rue Carnot, the present D 236, ran through the centre of Le Portel towards Equihen 12 kilometres to the south. It was the road nearest to the coast and was also at the junction of 2 and 3 Companies.

Drive on until you reach the next major junction and turn left onto the Boulevard de la Liberté signposted 'Boulogne A16'. After 100 metres or so park the car on the hard standing on your right.

This road, now the D236E to Etaples and Le Touquet, is the exact route of the light railway which in 1940 ran from the docks in Boulogne to its terminus in Le Portel. Note how the road sweeps round to the left and begins to descend on its way down to the port. This road marks the line of the withdrawal of the Irish Guards though the streets of Outreau towards the port area.

Lieutenant Colonel Haydon sent Major Ross, his second in command to reconnoitre a new and shortened line of defence on the morning of 23 May. The section of the railway as it ran straight on downhill just after the left hand curve in front of you, formed the major part of the new line selected by Major Ross from which the battalion could cover the western and southern approaches to Boulogne on the west bank of the Liane. The Irish began the withdrawal to their new positions in gardens and houses on either side of this route at around 10.30 am and the bulk of the battalion was in position by 11.30 am minus 3 and 1 Companies which caught up a little later, 1 Company having had to disengage from close quarters combat without further serious loss. Captain McCausland's leadership during this manoeuvre was later recognised with the award of the Distinguished Service Order. Excluding his officers, McCausland lost sixty of the one hundred men under his command either killed, wounded or missing during the Boulogne fighting.

179

The view from the cliff tops at Le Portal, slightly to the rear of the right flank of 3 Company, 2 Irish Guards.

During the two hours or so that the Guards made their stand astride the line of this street they were fighting almost continuously. At around 1.00 pm Lieutenant Colonel Haydon ordered a further retirement towards the docks and the Irish began to fall back once more towards the quays. Some of the Irish Bren guns had to be left behind as the barrels had warped due to the heat or they had become clogged with dirt.

Return to the car and follow the road down into Boulogne. You are now following the line of the final Irish withdrawal down a 'fairly important street'. Some 800 metres beyond the bend the light railway joined a road which followed the same route as the one on which you are now travelling. Imagine columns of disciplined Irish guardsmen marching down the road in front of you with some of the street corners covered by Bren guns and Boys anti-tank rifles. Imagine the area being pounded by German shells and then listen for the rattle of tank tracks in the silence as the bombardment lifts.

Five German tanks lumbered slowly down a street in this area led by a man in civilian clothes who proclaimed that the tanks were French as the Irish watched from nearby houses. In one house a French civilian was reported to have entered the back door of a house and flung himself on the floor as tank rounds thundered through the house above the heads of the guardsmen who had also hit the deck.

Looking south from a position on the cliffs above the hoverport at Le Portel. Note the entrance to the Avé Maria railway tunnel in the centre of the picture. Here the men of 3 Company dug their trenches and fox holes.

Eventually all five tanks returned up the hill and disappeared. In this area too Lieutenant J D Hornung the intelligence officer, saw two 'very small' tanks – probably PzKpfw 1's – sweep up a street as a guardsman managed to get off a quick shot with an anti-tank rifle. He scored a direct hit on the rear of one of the tanks, but as small as the tank was the shot appeared to have had no effect at all.

At around 3.00 pm on 23 May Lieutenant Colonel Haydon ordered a final move to the port. The Guards moved off and Sergeant William Gilchrist continued to protect the battalion's 'tail' as he had during most of the afternoon. He held a post at a street corner in this area with an anti-tank rifle for the better part of two hours under heavy machine gun fire. On another street corner not far away Lance Corporal Ivan Burke also succeeded in holding off the Germans by operating both a Bren gun and an anti-tank rifle until he had collapsed, partly due to exhaustion and partly due to concussion from a shell landing close by. Both men were decorated for their actions that day; Gilchrist with the award of the Distinguished Conduct Medal and Burke the Military Medal.

Continue down the hill and pass the village boundary sign for Boulogne-sur-mer. At the major junction ahead the road bends sharp right as you follow signs for 'A16 and A26.' Turn left immediately onto the Boulevard Auguste Huguet. This continues the line of the old railway down to the port area.

After some 500 metres turn right at the roundabout onto the Rue Huret Lagache and drive past the Findus factory as far as you can towards one of the inner harbour basins known as the Bassin Napoléon – once known as the Bassin a Flot. You will see the Gare Maritime across the water and the Basilica of the Haute Ville in the distance. **Turn right** – the enormous Findus France factory is still to your right – **at the end of the road onto the Boulevard du Bassin Naploéon. It is possible to park the car after 200-300 metres and to walk onto the Quay R Masset.** Please beware of industrial traffic crossing the quays and roads here.

This was the final destination of 2 Irish Guards after they had completed their withdrawal through Outreau. It was in this area on the quaysides that Lieutenant Colonel Haydon's men barricaded all the approach roads with vehicles and barrels and set up posts to cover them with automatic weapons whilst the majority took cover inside sheds and warehouses and waited patiently. When the destroyers finally arrived to evacuate 20 Brigade on the evening of 23 May the Irish impressed many of the naval officers on board with their discipline whilst waiting to board. There was no panic or rushing the gangplanks as the Irish boarded the *Venomous* and the *Wild Swan*. Imagine the scene on the *Quai Chanzy* as a number of the Irish fell into the water and had to be fished out by the sailors. Imagine the Bren gun squads which had been covering the embarkation thundering toward the ship at the double as HMS *Wild Swan* made ready to cast off at around 9.30 pm, whilst the

View across the Bassin Napoléon to the Gare Maritime from the quay R. Masset.

ship's gunners fired over open sights at anything that moved on the quays where you are standing.

For a German's eye view of the final positions of Major Windsor-Lewis at the Gare Maritime look across the Bassin. Two German tanks were positioned on this quay and fired across at the small force defending the harbour station. It was also from here that a small force of Germans attempted to attack the Gare Maritime by using small boats to cross the water in front of you on the evening of 24 May. The effort was repulsed.

Return to the car and drive on passing the Rue de Nemours on your right. Take the next right into the Rue Ferdinand Farjon. At the junction turn sharp left – you will see a concrete barrier in front of you. You must obey all the road signs at this point which was the site of the old Central Railway Station in 1940. After driving across the railway line filter into the traffic but keep to the left lane and after some 100 metres turn left and cross the Pont de l'Entente Cordiale, taking the left at the traffic lights on the other side of the bridge to return to the tourist office on the Boulevard Gambetta.

TOUR 3

From the German Assault on Fort de la Creche to the Final Stand at the Gare Maritime

This tour begins by tracing the line of the German assault on the French held Fort de la Creche on the high ground overlooking Boulogne to the north and then follows the German advance down into the town via the French positions near the Tour d'Odre on the cliff top overlooking the port. It ends at the harbour itself which was the scene of the evacuation of 20 Guards Brigade on the evening of 23 May and the final stand of a small mixed force under the command of Major Jim Windsor-Lewis, 2 Welsh Guards, which held off the Germans from 24 -25 May until finally overwhelmed.

From the Tourist Office at 24 Boulevard Gambetta drive south past the Pont Marguet, along the Boulevard de la Poste and take a left turn opposite the next bridge, the Pont de l'Entente Cordiale. Drive up the Grande Rue heading towards the Haute Ville and, keeping the ramparts to your right, follow signs for St. Omer at the traffic lights near the Porte de Calais. At the next major set of lights bear left along the Avenue Charles de Gaulle which, after a short distance, becomes the Route de Calais. After a little over one kilometre turn left at a junction on to the Rue de l'Aiglon. Turn right after a further 375 metres onto the Rue Napoléon and you will see the Colonne de la Grande Armée eventually come into view on your left. Park the car near the column.

This column topped by the figure of Napoleon Bonaparte rises to a height of fifty-four metres and commemorates a famous page in the history of Boulogne when the Emperor chose the town as the base for his Grande Armée intended for the invasion of Britain between 1803 and 1805. The Camp of Boulogne was in fact divided into two huge camps: the 'camp de droite', here, in and around the valley of Terlincthun and the plateau above the port near the Tour d'Odre, and the 'camp gauche' on the left bank of the Liane towards Outreau.

Look to your right down the long, tree lined Avenue de Colonne. It was in this avenue that *Oberleutnant* Durkes commanding 3 Platoon of the German 2 Motorcycle Battalion, 2 Panzer Division, woke up on the morning of May 23 under the shadow of Napoleon's column. He and *Oberst* von Vaerst, commanding 2 Schützen Brigade, climbed the 265 steps of the column to view the ground towards Fort de la Creche, Durkes' objective that morning. At 10.00 am German time the German artillery which had been brought into position in this area, had opened fire on the fort and under cover of a smoke screen Durkes' dismounted motorcyclists had ridden down the open 1000 metre slope to the railway at Terlincthun on the back of panzers. The park around the column is open to the public but do check times with the tourist office in advance. Opening times are also posted on the gates to the park.

The Colonne de la Grand Armée.

Return to the car and retrace your tracks. Turn right at the main road and follow the D96E towards Terlincthun. You are now moving in the direction of the German tanks carrying the dismounted motorcyclists as they advanced towards Fort de la Creche. Note the slope and imagine the German infantry hanging on to

183

the tanks for dear life as they bucked and reared over the ground. At least one man was seen to fall off and one tank shed a machine gun mounting.

Terlincthun CWGC military cemetery is to your right just before the junction with the D96. **Turn left onto the D96 and after some 500 metres park on the wide verge opposite the high grassy bank to your right.** Look back towards the Colonne Napoléon and the slope down which the German panzers came. *Oberleutnant* Durkes and his men had made an assault on the fort the previous evening. On that occasion the attack had been repulsed but on the morning of 23 May Durkes' men had dismounted from the panzers at the railway line which runs along the valley bottom and advanced under machine-gun fire across the field which slopes away to the south below you. Durkes and nine of his comrades took cover in a concrete well in the middle of the field, still marked on the IGN map although access is difficult as it is on private, cultivated land. Advancing behind a panzers Durkes was up to the fort and one of his men, Ascheraden, was cutting away the protective wire on the other side of the road from where you are now standing, within fifteen minutes of the start of the attack. Minutes later Durkes, *Unteroffizier* Weber and the rest of his men were inside. The French were so surprised by the speed of the assault that the Germans were waiting for the French gunners as they queued on the stairways of their bunkers trying to get out. All the officers were captured together and the rest of the fort was then 'combed out' and the position consolidated. Durkes estimated that they had taken sixteen officers and about 300 men prisoner. General Guderian later visited the captured fort to see it for himself.

This, the site of the original French fort, was the German Creche I position codenamed 'Blucher' during the occupation. The bunkers of the Creche II position – 'Arnika' – stud the cliffs on the other side of the D940 towards Wimereux, whilst Creche III was sited on the Pointe de la Creche just across the D940. The German Marine Artillerie Abteilung 240 (MAA 240) held the entire Creche position.

An eerie atmosphere pervades this rather remote spot today even in broad daylight. Spread over a large, roughly rectangular area it is possible to wander around the older brick built parts of the fort constructed by the French (note the date 1879 above one of the doorways) and see the concrete structures added by the German engineers and used by 3 Company of MAA 240 under the command of *Korvettekapitän* M A Fritz Diekmann who held this site. As you circle the three immense concrete casemates, note that after 1942 those gaping mouths were filled with large calibre coastal guns. The original French guns were of 194mm but the calibre of the German guns is in dispute. Some researchers claim that the German guns in the casemates were also 194mm whilst others argue that they were of 220mm. Other researchers claim that neither a 194mm nor 220mm gun would fit into this type of 'SK bunker'. The argument is ongoing with researchers still checking the data. Whatever the calibre these huge pieces were augmented with four 105mm guns in open emplacements (three of them in the fields behind the fort), one Bofors 28mm Flak and four 75mm Flak guns. In some accounts it is claimed that two Vickers 94mm AA heavy canons were situated in open positions on the cliff. Four MG 34 machine-guns were sited around the site to enfilade the access routes. The old fort, and its associated positions was perhaps the toughest nut of 'Festung Boulogne' – the town having acquired fortress status in Hitler's list of January 19 1944 – and was one of the last to fall to Canadian forces at 7.50 am 22 September 1944 during 'Operation Wellhit', the struggle to liberate the town. The impact marks made by bullets, shells and the damage from bombs dropped by seventy-eight medium bombers of the RAF on 21 September 1944 are clearly visible on the concrete emplacements.

(Please note that whilst the German 'Creche 2 and 3' positions are supervised by a French organisation named Eden 62, the 'Creche One' site is owned by the Conservatoire du Littoral, and at the time of writing – January 2002 – is a restricted area for security reasons, however, a group of French and Belgian historians led by team leader Robert Dehon, have joined forces to launch The Project la Creche (PLC) and are hoping to research the site and eventually establish it as an open air museum. Discussions between the project members and officials from the town councils of Boulogne, Wimereux and Le Portel have already taken place and a field survey has been completed to establish the site. 'Creche One' is scheduled to be open to the general public in July 2002 as a 'promenade' museum and the PLC team is working towards a full 'open air' museum to be opened in July 2004. The two dates chosen for the 'grand openings' are closely related with Boulogne's Napoleonic heritage. The project members are still concentrating on mapping and researching the history of the site. If all goes to plan the esplanade behind the German bunkers will be used for military re-enactments. If readers want to get a 'feel' of what La Crèche was like in the nineteenth century, they should visit Fort d'Alprech in Le Portel which has been renovated during the last few years. Fort d'Alprech is a twenty minute drive from La Creche over the Liane through Outreau to Le Portel – take the Rue du Cap off the D 236 Boulevard du General de Gaulle – and although not covered in detail by this guide Fort Alprech was held by French forces and finally fell to the Germans at around midday on 23 May. The area around the fort had in fact become untenable the previous day and the garrison had withdrawn to positions near the Casino. There are spectacular views over the Channel from Fort d'Alprech and many concrete German bunkers can be seen in the surrounding fields.

Look south towards Boulogne from Fort de la Creche and the port and note how the old Fort would have dominated the seaward approaches to the harbour. Note also that although the French had tried to spike their guns in 1940, a veteran German *Hauptfeldwebel* known as 'John' managed to bring one of them back into action on the evening of 23 May and used it to join other German artillery in firing on HMS *Venetia* as she came into port to evacuate 20 Guards Brigade. The *Venetia* was hit and set on fire and had to leave the harbour stern first without taking a

Fort d' Alprech in Le Portel. A twenty minute drive from Fort de la Creche.

single man on board.

Return to the car and drive on to the roundabout. Turn left along the D940 and head downhill towards Boulogne. After approximately 600 metres turn left onto the road leading to the Monument de la Légion d'Honneur and park the car near the monument. The stone obelisk marks the exact site of the throne on which Napoleon sat on August 16, 1804 for the first open air distribution of the Legion of Honour. Look north-east and note the vast natural amphitheatre created by the Terlincthun valley and how Napoleon's throne would have been at the very heart of the proceedings. 80,000 French troops were drawn up in an immense semi-circle on the slopes to the north-east – the same slopes traversed by the German panzers in 1940 as they attacked Fort de la Creche – and crowds of spectators joined them to witness 2,000 men receive their decorations from the Emperor himself.

Retrace your tracks back to the D 940 and turn left. After some 250 metres take a left turn onto the Rue d'Ambleteuse and then turn right after 800 metres onto the Rue de la Tour d'Odre. Park the car. You are now on the cliff top plateau with commanding views of the harbour and the village of Outreau on the opposite bank of the Liane. On a clear day the English coast can be seen clearly. The road is named after the Tour d'Odre an ancient lighthouse which collapsed in the Seventeenth Century due to the crumbling of the surrounding cliffs. Look seaward and note the squat building in a small depression surrounded by a low wall and fence. This is the restored Napoleonic Poudriere, the powder room or magazine in which could be stored up to 12,000 kilograms of gunpowder during the time of the Camp de Boulogne. Along with the column of the *Grande Armée* and the obelisk commemorating the Legion of Honour the Poudriere is one of the last vestiges of Boulogne's Napoleonic and Imperial heritage.

Walk a little further towards the large cross ahead. This is the Calvaire des Marins which now stands next to the sailor's chapel built in the shape of a ship. Both the cross and the original chapel also suffered at the hands of cliff top erosion but the cross was saved and now stands next to the mariners' chapel which was rebuilt in 1996.

The spot where you are standing is now known as the Place du Premier Maitre l'Her. During 23 May 1940 this area was the scene of bitter hand-to-hand fighting as the Germans tried to wrest control of this key position from a small French force of 200 men under *Commandant* Henri Nomy. *Premiere Maitre* Jean François L'Her was defending the position, still marked as the 'semaphore' on the IGN map, a little way back along the cliff top towards the Poudriere. *Premiere Maitre* L'Her, along with six other marines and one soldier, was killed during the fighting after he had himself shot a German soldier who had been trying to remove the French flag from the building. The entire position was finally taken at around 5.00 pm on 23 May, *Commandant* Nomy being taken prisoner with his surviving men. It was here in front of the Calvaire des Marins that a German officer is alleged to have threatened to shoot the survivors along with some French civilians who had been sheltering in the cellars of the semaphore building.

Look down from the platform of the post 1940 German bunker onto the harbour and note how the taking of this position gave the Germans almost total command of the harbour entrance and observation of movement on the quays. Note also the large and rather futuristic looking building below you on the Boulevard Ste Beuve. This is the French National Centre of the Sea – Nausicaa – which stands on the site of the old Casino. Look down and think of the small force of 200 French marines under the command of *Lieutenant de Vaisseau* de Saint Remy, which, with a lone 75mm gun, had blocked the coast road at the Casino. They managed to hold out all day on 23 May but by the evening were almost out of ammunition and albeit surrounded. They continued to resist until after 1.30 pm on 24 May when they at last tried to withdraw to the Haute Ville. Think also of the fifty men of Lieutenant Colonel Deane's AMPC on the extreme left flank of the British line astride the coast road a little way in advance of the Casino who, along with the remnants of 5 Buffs commanded by Major Penlington, had erected roadblocks using abandoned lorries and cars and the furniture from bombed out houses. The Germans probed their positions during the early hours of 23 May but withdrew only to return shortly afterwards with light tanks. With no anti-tank weapons the mixed British force watched as the leading tank climbed the first barricade which had been drenched in petrol. As soon as the tank's nose rose to an angle at which it could not fire its guns the defenders set the roadblock alight, at which point the tank reversed out of trouble. Under cover of the pall of smoke the Buffs and the AMPC hurriedly constructed a new barricade and fortunately for them the attack was not repeated. Note that these men were also being fired on from the quaysides to their rear as nervous and inexperienced troops from a variety of regiments and AMPC personnel awaiting evacuation on the opposite side of the harbour fired at anything that moved in the town. This was a problem which also plagued 20 Brigade during the final scenes of withdrawal.

Return to the car and take the left turn onto the Rue de Baron Bucaille at the calvary and drive to the junction with the Rue du Campe de Droite. Turn right again and drive towards the town until you reach the junction with the Rue Faidherbe. Turn right and park the car on the quayside in the parking spaces along either the Quai Gambetta or south of the Pont Marguet. Walk across the Pont Marguet towards the old Hoverspeed ferry terminal at the harbour station, the Gare Maritime. You are now following in the footsteps of the men of 1, 2 and 4 Companies of 2 Welsh Guards between 7.00 pm and 8.00 pm on 23 May as they crossed the bridge under the watchful eyes of both Lieutenant Colonel Alexander Stanier and Brigadier Fox-Pitt after Fox-Pitt had received the order to evacuate. 3 Company which had not received the order to withdraw, had not appeared and so Fox-Pitt ordered the bridge to be blown, albeit rather unsuccessfully. Those men of Colonel Dean's AMPC holding eight road blocks in the town were also left on the other side. Colonel Dean's car engine was riddled by bullets as he crossed this bridge before it was blown on the afternoon of 23 May to visit Brigadier Fox-Pitt to try to get him to stop the promiscuous firing from the 'odds and sods' milling around the Gare Maritime.

Note to your left front the church on top of the hill in the village of Outreau and the slope down which the Irish Guards withdrew to the harbour. As you reach the other side of the bridge note that the railway lines still run up to the Gare Maritime as they did in 1940. Cross the road and then cross the railway (there used to be a blue sign guiding 'Seacat – pedestrians' in the right direction). Go through one gate, making sure to look both ways, cross the line and turn right after passing through another gate on the opposite side. Walk towards the old terminal (cross-Channel ferry traffic has now ceased) and reflect that here were sited a number of sheds in which the Welsh Guards assembled after crossing the bridge.

As quiet as it is today it is difficult to imagine the crush and confusion on the quays in 1940 with the scream of Stuka dive-bombers and explosions adding to the chaos. It was here that Captain Duncan, 2 Welsh Guards, was killed by a bomb

187

Looking from the top of the ramp above the Gare Maritime towards the Pont Marguet with the line of Windsor-Lewis's sand-bagged defences.

which fell yards away from Lieutenant Colonel Stanier and the Padre as all three scrambled for cover under a railway carriage. Such were the numbers of military personnel and civilians crowding onto these quays on the evening of 23 May that Lieutenant Colonel Stanier lost touch with two entire companies of his battalion (2 and 4) which had sheltered in sheds on what is now the Quai Thurot. They, too, were left behind and, after trying to make a break out in the direction of Etaples at midnight on 23 May. Many were captured over the following two days. Guardsman Syd Pritchard and a comrade left 4 Company to make their way back here at dawn on 24 May and joined Major Windsor-Lewis of 3 Company, 2 Welsh Guards who had also withdrawn to this position.

Cross the tracks again where you see a blue 'sortie' sign and follow the eastern quay, keeping the wooden fence to your left, until you pass under the blue and white ramps and enter the station itself. It was here that Major Windsor-Lewis collected together a small mixed force of Welsh and Irish Guards, AMPC, RE, stragglers from other British regiments and 120 French troops who had been left behind after the evacuation on the night of 23 May. He determined to make a final stand here. Putting civilians on the lower levels of the station building itself he organised his defences.

Cross carefully towards the terminal building and walk back along the platform with the rail tracks to right and left, passing a small white kiosk until you reach the very end of the raised platform. Look back towards the Pont Marguet bridge. You are now standing on almost the exact site of the 'snout' of Major Windsor-Lewis's sandbagged defence line which enclosed the entire station. In 1940 two trains were drawn up on the tracks to either side of you. One of them, a hospital train, was to your right and both Syd Pritchard and Doug Davies took cover behind the bogey wheels of its carriages as the Germans on the opposite side of the Bassin Napoléon to your right poured fire into the train. In their accounts written for the home audience and neutral parties after the fall of Boulogne, the Germans took a dim view of the use of the hospital train as a defensive position although there were no patients on board at the time.

Imagine a German tank directly in front of you positioned near the Pont Marguet firing in your direction and another three across the Bassin Napoléon to your right doing the same as countless mortar rounds and a hurricane of small arms fire comes at you from buildings across the water to both your right and left. It was from across the Bassin to your right that the Germans attempted an assault by boat on the evening of 24 May which was repelled by Windsor-Lewis's force. It was only a matter of time however, before Windsor-Lewis was forced to accept the inevitable. After withdrawing into the station proper behind you – with only glass cover overhead – at noon on 25 May under terrific fire and with civilian lives at stake and many wounded being 'knocked about', the Major finally surrendered at around 1.00 pm on 25 May in order to avoid a 'massacre'. The German troops swept past the spot where you are now standing and into the station where they treated the survivors with professional courtesy.

It is possible, with care, to access the western side of the old Hoverspeed terminal and walk up the vehicle ramp to the upper level from where, looking south, you will have an excellent view of the location of the final sandbagged position and the quays on the opposite side of the Bassin to the west on which the German panzers lined up to take pot shots at the garrison. Note the steep hill to the east up to the Haute Ville and St. Martin beyond and pick out the communications pylons on the heights of Mont Lambert between the apartment blocks on the Boulevard Gambetta. From this final position it is a sobering thought to reflect again on the enormity of the task given to two battalions with no transport to speak of when one considers the distance out towards Mont Lambert to the east and Outreau to the west.

Retrace your steps back towards the Pont Marguet, again watching out for any rail traffic when crossing the tracks at pedestrian crossing points, re-cross the bridge and return to the car parked on the opposite bank.

Bibliography

Bataille Guy, *Boulogne sur Mer 1939-1945* (Dunkerque: Westhoek Éditions, 1984.)

Borchert H, *Panzerkampf im Westen* (Berlin: 1940.)

Cras Hervé and **Mordal Jacques**, *Dunkerque* (Paris: Éditions France Empire, 1960.)

Ellis L.F., *The War in France & Flanders, 1939-40* (HMSO, 1953.)

Ellis Major L.F., *Welsh Guards at War, 1939-1946* (London Stamp Exchange, 1989.)

Evans Arthur, *Sojourn in Silesia* (Ashford: Ashford Writers, 1995.)

Fitzgerald Major D.J.L., *History of the Irish Guards in the Second World War* (Aldershot: Gale and Polden, 1952.)

Glover M, *The Fight for the Channel Ports* (London: Leo Cooper, 1985.)

Guderian Generaloberst, (Ed.) *Mit den Panzern in Ost und West*. Vol.i (Berlin: Volk und Reich, 1942.)

Hanbury Peter, *A Not Very Military Experience.* (Petersfield: Millstream, 2000.)

Künzel Oberleutnant, Einnahme von Boulogne-sur-Mer in *Militär-Wochenblatt*, No.35, Cols. 1517-1521. (Berlin, 1940.)

Rhodes-Wood Major E.H., *A War History of the Royal Pioneer Corps 1939-45* (Aldershot: Gale and Polden, 1960.)

Stanier Brigadier Sir Alexander Bt., DSO, MC., *Sammy's Wars.* (Privately published, 1998).

Steinzer Franz, *Die Friedens und Kriegsjahre der 2 (Wiener)Panzerdivision in Wort und Bild* (Privately published.)

Stoves Rolf, *Die gepanzerten und motorisierten deutschen Großverbände (Divisionen und selbständige Brigaden)1935-1945* (Friedberg 3: Podzun-Pallas, 1986.)

Strauß F.J., *Friedens und Kriegserlebnisse einer Generation.- Ein Kapitel Weltgeschichte aus der Sicht der Panzerjäger-Abteilung 38(SF) in der ehemaligen 2 (Wiener) Panzerdivision.* (Neckargemünd: Kurt Vowinkel, 1961.)

INDEX

3 Royal Tank Regiment,
    19,38,83.
1 Welsh Guards, 29,39,46.
2 Welsh Guards, *passim*
2 Searchlight Regiment,
    Royal Artillery, 50.
275 Anti-Tank Battery, Royal
    Artillery, 53.
69 Anti-Tank Regiment,
    Royal Artillery, 53.
2 Heavy Anti-Aircraft
    Regiment, Royal Artillery,
    50,53,99.
58 Light Anti-Aircraft
    Regiment, Royal Artillery,
    50.
262 Field Company, Royal
    Engineers, 76.
657 General Construction
    Company, Royal
    Engineers, 46.
5 Group Auxiliary Military
    Pioneer Corps (AMPC),
    50,76,83,99,100,103,
    136,138,143,145,187.

French Units
21 Infantry Division, 52,62,
    153,171.
Regiments:
    48 Infantry, 53,153.
    65 Infantry, 53,153.
    13 Regiment Regionale,
        150,172.
    417 Pioneer, 156.

German Units
XIX Panzer Corps, 8,23,
    63,111.
1 Panzer Division, 20,25,27.
2 Panzer Division, *passim*
7 Panzer Division, 76.
10 Panzer Division, 25,27.
2 Panzer Brigade, 63,64.
2 Schützen Brigade, 63,64,
    154,183.
2 Motorcycle Battalion,
    78,129,183.
3 Panzer Regiment, 130.
Panzer Pioneer Battalion 38, 79.
Tank Destroyer Battalion 38,
    64-66.

Ships
British:
    HMS *Keith*, 115,119,121-123.
    HMS *Venetia*, 129,130,133,185.
    HMS *Venomous*, 129,130,135-
        137,181.
    HMS *Verdun*, 173.
    HMS *Vimiera*, 43,123,126,
        128,129,138.
    HMS *Vimy*, 112,115,116, 120,
        122.
    HMS *Wild Swan*, 129,130,133,
        181.
    HMS *Windsor*,137-139.
    HMS *Whitshed*, 35,43-46,112-
        114,115-116,122,123,126,
        128,129.
    SS *Biarritz*, 39,41,43,46.
    SS *Mona's Star*, 41,43.
    SS *Queen of the Channel*, 43,47.

French:
    L'Orage, 112,121.
    Ophelie, 45.